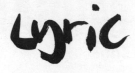

D0239184

MOGADISHU

by **Vivienne Franzmann**

A Royal Exchange Theatre, Manchester and Lyric Hammersmith Production

Winner of the 2008 Bruntwood Prize for Playwriting

The first performance of *Mogadishu* was at the
Royal Exchange Theatre, Manchester on 26 January 2011

The first performance of this production was at
Liverpool Playhouse on 30 January 2012

MOGADISHU

Tour 2012

Liverpool Playhouse / 30 Jan – 04 Feb
0151 709 4776 / www.everymanplayhouse.com

Cambridge Arts Theatre / 07 – 11 Feb
01223 503333 / www.cambridgeartstheatre.com

Oxford Playhouse / 14 – 18 Feb
01865 305305 / www.oxfordplayhouse.com

Warwick Arts Centre / 21 – 25 Feb
024 7652 4524 / www.warwickartscentre.co.uk

Royal & Derngate, Northampton / 28 Feb – 03 Mar
01604 624811 / www.royalandderngate.co.uk

Eastbourne Devonshire Park / 06 – 10 Mar
01323 412000 / www.eastbournetheatres.co.uk

Nuffield Theatre, Southampton / 13 – 15 Mar
023 8067 1771 / www.nuffieldtheatre.co.uk

Northern Stage, Newcastle / 20 – 24 Mar
0191 230 5151 / www.northernstage.co.uk

Lyric Hammersmith / 27 – 31 Mar
0871 22 117 22 / www.lyric.co.uk

MOGADISHU

by **Vivienne Franzmann**

Cast (in order of appearance)
Jason **Ryan Calais Cameron**
Chloe **Tara Hodge**
Saif **Farshid Rokey**
Chuggs **Tendayi Jembere**
Dee **Savannah Gordon-Liburd**
Jordon **Hammed Animashaun**
Firat **Michael Karim**
Amanda **Jackie Clune**
Becky **Rosie Wyatt**
Chris **James Barriscale**
Peter **Jason Barnett**
Ben **Nicholas Beveney**

Director **Matthew Dunster**
Designer **Tom Scutt**
Lighting Designer **Philip Gladwell**
Sound Designer **Ian Dickinson** for Autograph
Fight Director **Kev McCurdy**
Associate Director **Stef O'Driscoll**
Assistant Designer **Rachel Wingate**
Production Relighter **Rachel Bowen**
Sound Operator **Matt Russell**

Company Stage Manager **Fiona Kennedy**
Deputy Stage Manager **Rachael Presdee**
Assistant Stage Manager & Wardrobe Assistant **Sally C Roy**

Senior Producer **Imogen Kinchin**
Producer **Bailey Lock**
Production Manager **Seamus Benson**
Production Carpenter **Courtland Evje**

Cast

Ryan Calais Cameron Jason
Theatre includes: *The Westbridge* (Royal Court) and *Coyote Was Going There* (Lighthouse). **Film includes:** *Mad Frank* and *Yesterday's Tomorrow*.

Tara Hodge Chloe
Theatre includes: original production of *Mogadishu* (Royal Exchange Theatre, Manchester/Lyric Hammersmith); *Beautiful Thing* (Royal Exchange Theatre, Manchester); *Citizenship* (Young Actors' Theatre/Old Vic); *Two's A Company, Boogie Nights* and *The Shoemaker's Incredible Wife* (Young Actors' Theatre) and *Spiel Im Berg* (Absolute Theatre). **Film includes:** *Sunny Boy, Hitler and Henry, Veronica Guerin, French Exchange, F1rst, The Body, Baby Girl, Cubs, Forever Friends* and *The Kid.* **TV includes:** *Casualty, EastEnders E20, The Bill, The Brief, Midsomer Murders, The Garden, Argumental* and *Coming Down the Mountain.*

Farshid Rokey Saif
Theatre includes: original production of *Mogadishu* (Royal Exchange Theatre, Manchester/Lyric Hammersmith); *This Year will be Different* (Theatre503) and *In the Unlikely Event of an Emergency* (Soho). **Film includes:** *Undefeated, The Morning After the Night Before, Stolen Lives* and *Me and My Dad.* **TV includes:** *Doctors, The Fureys* and *The Endz.* **Radio includes:** *Mogadishu.*

Tendayi Jembere Chuggs
Theatre includes: original production of *Mogadishu* (Royal Exchange Theatre, Manchester/Lyric Hammersmith); *The Kitchen* (National Theatre); *Boy X* (Arc Theatre); *Angel House* (New Wolsey Theatre); *Circle of Life* (Clock Tower); *D.R.D.* (Stratford East); *Variety Show, C 4 Yourself, National Youth Musical Theatre Project, Girlz and Boyz* (Stratford Circus); *Big Breder* (Tour) and *Blaggers* (New Vic). **TV includes:** *The Bill, Dubplate Drama, Mr Harvey Lights a Candle, Doctors* and *Kerching!* **Radio includes:** *Mogadishu* and *Silver Street.*

Savannah Gordon-Liburd Dee
Theatre includes: original production of *Mogadishu* (Royal Exchange Theatre, Manchester/Lyric Hammersmith); *The Wiz* (Hackney Empire). **Film includes:** *My Brother the Devil* and *The Party*. **TV includes:** *One Night*, *EastEnders E20* and *The Sarah Jane Adventures*.

Hammed Animashaun Jordon
Theatre includes: original production of *Mogadishu* (Royal Exchange Theatre, Manchester/Lyric Hammersmith); *Aladdin* (Lyric Hammersmith); *Married to the Game* (Theatre503); *Seven New Plays* (Kids Company at National Theatre Studio); *Superhuman* (SPID Theatre); *Money and Rain*, *Othello*, *Tagged* and *Rudi* (Half Moon/Scriptworks). **Film includes:** *Tooting Broadway*, *The Ellington Kid*, *Twenty8K*, *Borrowed Time*, *Drift*, *God View* and *Affected*. **TV includes:** *Shine, Shine, Shine* and *A Life in the Knife of You?*

Michael Karim Firat
Theatre includes: original production of *Mogadishu* (Royal Exchange Theatre, Manchester/Lyric Hammersmith); *Skäne* (Hampstead Theatre); *An Evening with Harold Pinter* (Creative Team Productions); *Bugsy Malone*, *The Musicians*, *West Side Story*, *Cabaret*, *Oliver!* (RVHS) and *A Midsummer Night's Dream* (Shakespeare's School Festival). **Film includes:** *Truant* and *Three Kings*. **TV includes:** *Parents of the Band*. **Radio includes:** *Mogadishu*.

Jackie Clune Amanda
Theatre includes: *Mamma Mia* (UK and international tours); *Billy Elliot* (Victoria Palace); *Julie Burchill is Away* (Soho/Assembly Rooms, Edinburgh/Brighton Pavillion Theatre); *The Belle's Stratagem* (Southwark Playhouse); *Showstopper* (Assembly Rooms, Edinburgh/Arts Theatre); *A Wedding Story* (Birmingham Repertory Theatre/Soho); *The Vagina Monologues* (Ambassadors) and *Taboo* (Venue). **Cabaret includes:** *Boy Crazy* (Assembly Rooms, Edinburgh/Soho); *Bitchin'* (Assembly Rooms, Edinburgh/Arts Theatre); *It's Jackie!* (Assembly Rooms, Edinburgh/Drill Hall); *Follow the Star!* (Drill Hall) and *Chicks with Flicks* (Assembly Rooms, Edinburgh/King's Head/UK tour). **TV includes:** *Breathtaking*, *The Bill*, *EastEnders*, *Waking the Dead*, *Never Mind the Buzzcocks*, *The Staying in Show* and *QI*. **Radio includes:** *The Jackie Clune Show*, *Loose Ends*, *Jammin'* and *The Day the Music Died*. **Books include:** *Extreme Motherhood – The Triplet Diaries* and *Man of the Month Club*.

Rosie Wyatt Becky
Theatre includes: *Bunny* (Soho/Udderbelly, Edinburgh/UK tour/New York); *Love Love Love* (Paines Plough/tour) and *Whose Shoes* (National Youth Theatre). **TV includes:** *Doctors* and *Table Manners*. **Radio includes:** *The Blood of Strangers*.

James Barriscale Chris
Theatre includes: *War Horse* (National Theatre/West End); *St Joan* (National Theatre); *Hamlet* (English Touring Theatre/Donmar); *Twelfth Night, Zenobia, The Wives' Excuse, The Broken Heart, Redskin* and *Henry V* (RSC). **Film includes:** *Tuesday, The Birthday, Inferno, Diamond Lill, Navy in Action, When in London* and *Northern Lights*. **TV includes:** *Silent Witness, Spooks, Pulling, Murphy's Law, The Vice, Messiah, Cherished, England Expects, Dalziel and Pascoe, Kavanagh QC, A Touch of Frost, The Bill, Attachments, Rockface, Holby City, Diana: Last Days of a Princess, Little Devils, The Heat Surgeon, Big Women, Like Father Like Son* and *Casualty*.

Jason Barnett Peter
Theatre includes: *Pinter's Party Time, One for the Road* (JMK Award winner); *Jason and the Argonauts, The World Cup of 1966, Project D, I am Mediocre* (BAC); *Julius Caesar, Burn* (Synergy); *The Fixer* (Almeida); *Winged* (Tristan Bates/tour); *Come Out Eli* (Tristan Bates/tour; Time Out Best New Production); *Cruising* (Bush); *A Midsummer Night's Dream, All the Right People Come Here* (Wimbledon Theatre); *The Victorian in the Wall, The Girlfriend Experience* (Royal Court); *Days of Significance, Pericles, Winter's Tale* (RSC); *Amato Saltone* (National Theatre/Shunt) and *War Horse* (National Theatre). **Film includes:** *Rains of Fear, One Man and His Dog, Plotless* and *The Refugee*. **TV includes:** *Dead Ringers, Coming of Age, Fur TV, Little Britain, Stupid! Hotel Trubble, The Legend of Dick and Dom, Vivien Vyle, Doctors, Extras, The Bill* (nomination for Best Newcomer at Screen Nation 2008, RTS, BAFTA winning ensemble 2009).

Nicholas Beveney Ben
Theatre includes: *The Frontline, Bible Readings, Savage Sensuality* (Shakespeare's Globe); *La Dispute* (Abbey Theatre, Dublin); *Yours Abundantly* (Ovalhouse); *Macbeth* (Theatre Clwyd); *Blame* (Sphinx/York Theatre); *Sleeping Beauty* (Young Vic); *The Battle of Green Lanes* (Stratford East); *Ma Rainey's Black Bottom* (Liverpool Playhouse); *Bintou* (Arcola); *Silence* (Birmingham Repertory Theatre); *The Gift* (Birmingham Repertory Theatre/Tricycle); *Big Nose* (Belgrade, Coventry); *A Midsummer Night's Dream* (Oxford Stage Company) and *Wicked Games* (West Yorkshire Playhouse). **Film includes:** *Blacklands, Nowhere Man, ACG, Swinging with the Finkels, Spring Ritual, Dangerous Parking, Life in Lyrics, Sahara, The Fifth Element* and *Jack and the Beanstalk.* **TV includes:** *New Tricks, Law & Order, No. 1 Ladies' Detective Agency, Gunrush, Poppy Shakespeare, Casualty, This Life – 10 Years On, Skins, Waking the Dead, Doctor Who, Funland, Murder Prevention, Holby City, Sir Gadabout, Lock Stock, Trial & Retribution, The Bill, Pie in the Sky, Turning World* and *Sharman.* **Radio includes:** *Joys of War* and *The Grass is Singing.*

Creative Team

Vivienne Franzmann Writer
Theatre includes: *Mogadishu* (Royal Exchange Theatre, Manchester/Lyric Hammersmith; winner of the 2008 Bruntwood Playwriting Competition, George Devine Award 2010 and nominations for Most Promising Playwright at the Evening Standard Awards 2011 and for Best New Play at the Theatre Awards UK 2011 and Whatsonstage.com Awards 2012).
Current projects include: projects for Clean Break, Channel 4, Radio 4 and *The Witness* (Royal Court).

Matthew Dunster Director
Matthew is an associate artist at the Young Vic. **Theatre includes:** As Director: *Mogadishu* (Royal Exchange Theatre, Manchester/Lyric Hammersmith); *The Two Gentlemen of Verona* (Royal & Derngate, Northampton); *Saturday Night Sunday Morning, 1984, Macbeth* (Royal Exchange Theatre, Manchester); *Doctor Faustus, The Frontline* (Shakespeare's Globe); *Love the Sinner* (National Theatre); *Love and Money* (Royal Exchange Theatre, Manchester/Young Vic); *Testing the Echo* (Out of Joint); *The Member of the Wedding, Some Voices* (Young Vic); *Cruising* (Bush); *Project D: I'm Mediocre* (The Work) and *Port Authority* (Liverpool Everyman). As Writer: *Children's Children* (Almeida); *The Most Incredible Thing* (Sadler's Wells) and *You Can See the Hills* (Royal Exchange Theatre, Manchester/Young Vic).

Tom Scutt Designer
Theatre includes: *Mogadishu* (Royal Exchange Theatre, Manchester/Lyric Hammersmith); *Absent Friends* (West End); *13* (National Theatre); *Romeo and Juliet, The Merchant of Venice* (RSC); *King Lear, Through a Glass Darkly* (Almeida); *Constellations, Remembrance Day* (Royal Court); *Aladdin, Dick Whittington and his Cat, Jack and the Beanstalk* (Lyric Hammersmith); *Realism* (Soho); *South Downs/The Browning Version* (Chichester Festival Theatre); *Hamlet* (Sheffield Crucible); *Pressure Drop* (On Theatre); *After Miss Julie* (Salisbury); *A Midsummer Night's Dream, Edward Gant's Amazing Feats of Loneliness* (Headlong Theatre); *Here Lies Mary Spindler, The 13 Midnight Challenges of Angelus Diablo* (RSC at Latitude); *The Contingency Plan: On the Beach/Resilience* (Bush); *Vanya, Unbroken* and *The Internationalist* (Gate); *Bay* (Young Vic); *The Merchant of Venice* (Octagon); *Metropolis* (Bath); *The Observer* (Design Consultant, National Theatre Studio); *Paradise Lost* (Southwark); *Mad Funny Just, The Water Harvest* (Theatre 503); *Return* (Watford) and *The Comedy of Errors* (RSC/RWCMD). **Opera includes:** *Rigoletto* (Opera Holland Park).
Tom received a 2007 Linbury Biennial Prize for his work with Headlong Theatre and also the 2007 Jocelyn Herbert Award.

Philip Gladwell Lighting Designer
Theatre includes: *Mogadishu* (Royal Exchange Theatre, Manchester/Lyric Hammersmith); *Love the Sinner* (National Theatre); *The King and I* (number one UK tour); *Punk Rock* (Royal Exchange Theatre, Manchester/Lyric Hammersmith); *Aladdin* (Lyric Hammersmith); *The Two Gentlemen of Verona* (Royal & Derngate, Northampton); *You Can't Take It With You, 1984, Macbeth* (Royal Exchange Theatre, Manchester); *Rigoletto, La Wally* (Opera Holland Park); *Amazonia, Ghosts, The Member of the Wedding, Festa!* (Young Vic); *Radio Times, Relatively Speaking, Daisy Pulls It Off* (Watermill Theatre); *Miss Julie* (Berlin); *Five Guys Named Moe* (Underbelly/Theatre Royal Stratford); *After Dido* (ENO); *Così fan tutte* (WNO); *My Romantic History* (Bush); *Origins, For Once* (Pentabus); *Terminus* (Abbey/tour); *The Wiz* (Birmingham Repertory Theatre/West Yorkshire Playhouse); *Harvest* (UK tour); *Oedipus Rex* (Royal Festival Hall); *Oxford Street, Kebab* (Royal Court); *Il trittico* (Opera Zuid); *Testing the Echo* (Out of Joint); *Falstaff* (Grange Park Opera); *Design for Living, Low Pay? Don't Pay!* (Salisbury Playhouse); *Dandy in the Underworld, Shraddha, Overspill, HOTBOI, Tape* (Soho); *Melody, In the Bag* (Traverse) and *Mother Courage and Her Children* (UK tour). Philip was recently nominated by the UK Theatre Awards for Best Lighting Design for *The Duchess of Malfi* (Theatre Royal, Northampton) and by the Off West End Awards for Best Lighting Design for *Mogadishu* at the Lyric.

Ian Dickinson Sound Designer
Theatre includes: *Mogadishu* (Royal Exchange Theatre, Manchester/Lyric Hammersmith); *Haunted Child* (Royal Court); *13, Season's Greetings, After the Dance, Women Beware Women, Our Class, All's Well That Ends Well, Death and the King's Horseman, Harper Regan, The Hothouse, Pillars of the Community* (National Theatre); *South Downs/The Browning Version* (Chichester Festival Theatre); *Top Girls* (Chichester Festival Theatre/Trafalgar Studios); *Two Gentlemen of Verona* (Royal & Derngate, Northampton); *Jerusalem* (Apollo Theatre/Broadway; Olivier and Tony Award nominations); *Betrayal, The Misanthrope* (Comedy Theatre); *Cause Celebre* (Old Vic); *Don Giovanni* (ENO); *John Gabriel Borkman* (Abbey Theatre, Dublin/BAM, New York); *Pieces of Vincent* (Arcola); *Little Voice* (Vaudeville); *A Delicate Balance, Mrs Klein* (Almeida); *1984, Macbeth, Love and Money* (Royal Exchange Theatre, Manchester); *A Few Good Men* (Haymarket); *Spur of the Moment, Wig Out!, Now or Later, Gone Too Far!, Rhinoceros, My Child, The Seagull, Krapp's Last Tape, Drunk Enough To Say I Love You?, Piano/Forte, Rock 'n' Roll* (Olivier and Tony Award nominations), *Motortown, The Winterling, Alice Trilogy, Fewer Emergencies, Way to Heaven, The Woman Before, stoning mary, Breathing Corpses, Dumb Show, Shining City, Lucky Dog, Ladybird, Notes on Falling Leaves, Loyal Women, The Sugar Syndrome, Blood, Playing the Victim, Fallout, Flesh Wound, Hitchcock Blonde, Black Milk, Crazyblackmuthafuckin'self, Caryl Churchill Shorts, Push Up, Fucking Games, Herons* (Royal Court); *Othello, Much Ado About Nothing, Night of the Soul* and *The Whore's Dream* (RSC).

Kev McCurdy Fight Director

Theatre includes: *Mogadishu* (Royal Exchange Theatre, Manchester/Lyric Hammersmith); *Batman Live World Arena Tour* (Warner Bros); *Romeo and Juliet* (Headlong Theatre); *Of Mice and Men, The Grapes of Wrath* (Cymru Theatr Clwyd); *Quadrophenia* (UK tour); *Beauty and The Beast* (Sherman Theatre Cardiff); *It's Not the End of the World, Cyrano De Bergerac, Suspension* (Bristol Old Vic); *We The People, The Frontline, Troillus and Cressida, Bedlam, Helen, Macbeth* (Shakespeare's Globe); *Die Fledermaus, Il Trovatore, Don Giovanni* (WNO); *Electra, Dream Story* (Gate Theatre); *The Heart of Robin Hood, Marat Sade* (RSC); *Treasure Island, As You Like It* (Rose Theatre); *Cause Célèbre* (Old Vic) and *Broken Glass* (Tricycle/Vaudeville Theatres). **Film includes:** *John Carter of Mars, Season of the Witch* and *Panic Button*. **TV includes:** *Doctor Who Christmas Special, Torchwood, Becoming Human, Belonging, Young Dracula, The Story of Tracy Beaker, Hearts of Gold, Camelot, Pobol Y Cwm, Y Pris, Caerdydd, Pen Taler, Gwaith Cyntaf* and *Alys*.

Thanks to:
Andy Stubbs
Karin Anderson

Blasted

Ghost Stories

Punk Rock

Aladdin

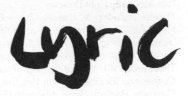

The Lyric Hammersmith is one of the UK's leading producing theatres.

For over a hundred years, we have welcomed some of the world's finest writers, directors, actors and theatre companies to our stages. From Harold Pinter to Simon Stephens; Sir John Gielgud to Robert Lepage; Complicite to Frantic Assembly.

Following the success of *Mogadishu* at the Royal Exchange Theatre, Manchester and the Lyric Hammersmith in 2011, we have remounted the show for a major UK tour. Other recent Lyric tours include the award-winning *Punk Rock* and *Three Sisters*.

We hope you enjoy the show.

www.lyric.co.uk

Sean Holmes Artistic Director
Jessica Hepburn Executive Director

Photos: Helen Maybanks, Simon Kane and Tristram Kenton

supported by

h&f
hammersmith & fulham

Supported by

ARTS COUNCIL
ENGLAND

Royal
Exchange
Theatre

The Royal Exchange Theatre, Manchester is one of the leading theatres in the UK. Producing a repertoire of up to twelve productions a year in our 750-seat permanent theatre-in-the-round and the 100-seat Studio, we are passionate about what our theatre can offer. We aim to present great writing in quality productions that tell intimate and epic stories that entertain, provoke and inspire. We collaborate with some of the most innovative and original theatremakers in this country. We work in partnership with different communities to help them express themselves creatively. We train, develop and mentor future generations of theatre artists and make our building a place for people to meet, talk, work and relax in the heart of the vibrant city of Manchester.

Braham Murray, Greg Hersov and Sarah Frankcom **Artistic Directors**
Fiona Gasper **Executive Director**

The Great Hall of the Royal Exchange

Royal Exchange Theatre, St. Ann's Square, Manchester M2 7DH
www.royalexchange.co.uk   +44 161 833 9333

 **AGMA**
ASSOCIATION OF
GREATER MANCHESTER
AUTHORITIES

 MANCHESTER
CITY COUNCIL

 Supported by
**ARTS COUNCIL
ENGLAND**

Registered Charity Number 255424

MOGADISHU

Vivienne Franzmann

Acknowledgements

My thanks to everyone at the Royal Exchange Manchester, Bruntwood and the Lyric, all the actors involved and everyone that offered their experiences, opinions and support. Extra-special thanks to Matthew Dunster for the wise words and all the encouragement.

Vivienne Franzmann

For Kev

4

Characters

JASON, *fifteen, leader, black*
JORDON, *fifteen, Chloe's best friend, black*
SAIF, *fifteen, Chuggs' best friend, Asian Muslim*
CHUGGS, *fifteen, Saif's best friend, black*
CHLOE, *fifteen, a big gob, white*
DEE, *fifteen, Jason's girl, more serious than most, black*
FIRAT, *fourteen, recently arrived from Turkey*
AMANDA, *Becky's mum, forties, English teacher, white*
BECKY, *fourteen, eyeliner and wristbands, white*
CHRIS, *head teacher, fifties, white*
PETER, *Amanda's husband, forties, IT support worker, black*
BEN, *Jason's father, forties, security guard, black*

Location

A school in London

This text went to press before the end of rehearsals and so may differ slightly from the play as performed.

ACT ONE

Scene One

Under the stairs. School. A small space somewhere between in and out, public and private. JASON is smoking. Around him are his attendants; JORDON, SAIF, CHUGGS, CHLOE and DEE. They are laughing and pissing about. JASON is in charge. An explosion of laughter; JASON pushes JORDON, who falls into CHLOE. She shrieks lots of 'fuck you', 'gay', 'fucking prick'. A bit of shoving and pushing, all good-humoured enough. FIRAT walks down the stairs, sees the group, goes to turn around, looks at his watch, thinks he will be late, reconsiders and hurries past them; but in the pissing about, JASON knocks into him and FIRAT falls onto him. JASON burns himself on his joint.

JASON. What the fuck?

FIRAT. Sorry.

JASON. What you doing, man?

FIRAT. Sorry.

JASON. You burnt me. You fuckin' burnt me.

FIRAT. Yes. Yes. Sorry.

JASON. He burnt me. He fuckin' burnt me.

FIRAT. It was accident.

JASON. You burnt a hole in my top.

FIRAT. Sorry.

JASON. This is my favourite top, innit.

JORDON. It is. He wears it all the time.

FIRAT. You bumped me.

JORDON. From Nike Town.

CHUGGS. You bummed him.

JORDON (*to* CHLOE). I got the same one in blue, like a duck-egg blue. Sick.

CHUGGS. Did you hear what he said? Jas, you bummed him.

Laughter.

FIRAT. I said sorry. What do you want me to do?

CHUGGS. He said he bummed him.

JASON. I want you to go back in time and not to have burnt a hole in my bare fuckin' expensive Nike top.

FIRAT. Don't be silly billy.

Barely suppressed sniggers from the others. JASON, embarrassed, starts to laugh.

JASON (*laughing*). You's out of order. Who the fuck do you think you are? This is my favourite fuckin' top and you burnt a fuckin' hole in it. Callin' me a silly billy. He's callin' me a fuckin' silly billy.

FIRAT (*noting change in atmosphere, smiles and wags his finger*). You should not smoke in school.

JASON. Don't tell me what to do, innit.

FIRAT. Get cancer. In your lungs.

JASON. Don't tell me what to do, you cunt.

Pause.

Arab cunt.

FIRAT. Please do not say that.

JASON. Paki cunt.

FIRAT. You are racist.

JASON. Do you know me? Do you know anything about me?

FIRAT. You said I was an Arab C U Next Tuesday. You said –

JASON. You burnt my top.

FIRAT. Yes. I have said sorry.

JASON. You are a fuckin' hoodie-burning, Arab terrorist bomb-making Muslim fuckin' cunt.

FIRAT. I tire of this.

As he goes to walk away, JASON *grabs him. The others are excited by it all.* FIRAT *is pushed to the floor.* JASON *is now furious.* DEE *goes to pull him away, he pulls away from her. Lots of noise. Pulling back, pushing forward.* FIRAT *on his hands and knees trying to straighten his glasses, picking up his books and his briefcase.* JASON *holding onto him, hitting him, nasty, meaning it.* AMANDA *comes down the stairs. She sees the fight and immediately rushes forward to stop it. She pushes her way through them.*

AMANDA. Stop it. Boys!

The others cheer and shout, stoking it up, taking no notice of her.

Stop it. Jason, get off him. (*She tries to pull* JASON *away.*) Get off him. (*To the others.*) Don't just stand there. Get off him. Jason!

They take no notice of her.

JASON. You pussy. I'll cut you up.

AMANDA. That's enough.

She gets in between them. FIRAT *is on the floor trying to get away.*

JASON. Chattin' shit. Watch. Watch.

AMANDA. Jason, that's enough.

JASON. Watch. You fuckin' Paki cunt, Muslim cunt.

AMANDA. Stop it. I said stop it!

JASON. Fuck you.

JASON, full of rage, pushes AMANDA *out of the way. She falls to the floor. The rest stop and look at her. Shock.* DEE *goes to* AMANDA. SAIF *stops her.* AMANDA *sits up.* JASON *feels the change in atmosphere. He turns round sees her on the floor. Registers what has happened. He looks at* AMANDA. *He looks at* FIRAT. *He turns and walks slowly away from the scene, followed by the rest of the group trying to appear casual, not worried, bopping.* DEE *stares at her.*

FIRAT *gets up, trying to straighten his glasses. Puts them on and then looks at* AMANDA, *at* DEE, *back at* AMANDA.

DEE. Miss?

Pause.

Miss?

AMANDA *starts getting up. She doesn't look at them.* FIRAT *stares, horrified.*

AMANDA. Get to class.

They both look at her.

Now.

Scene Two

AMANDA*'s house. Her daughter* BECKY *is with her.* BECKY *wears the same school uniform as the previous kids.* AMANDA *is sitting at her dining-room table nursing a large glass of wine.* BECKY *is sitting on the kitchen countertop and picking at a piece of toast.*

BECKY. He's such a wanker.

AMANDA. Rebecca, please.

BECKY. In primary, he begged Mrs Stapleton to let him take the school hamster home for the holiday and when he brought it back, it had this horrible burn mark on its fur, like a cigarette or something. And of course, no one made a fuss, just acted as if this was totally fucking normal.

AMANDA. Please stop swearing.

BECKY. Well, they fucking did, like it was no big deal that a hamster had been abused on its holiday.

AMANDA *starts laughing.*

It's not funny, Mum.

AMANDA. You're right, animals should not be abused while they're on holiday.

BECKY. Stop taking the piss. Animal cruelty is no laughing matter.

AMANDA. True.

BECKY. Imagine if it had been someone else that had brought it back in that condition. If I went in and said, 'Morning, Mrs Stapleton, I've brought back Hammy the Hamster, the school symbol of nurture, care and collective responsibility. Oh, sorry about his foot. Yes, it is a bloody stump. I just wanted to see what would happen if I tried to cut it off.

Pause.

Oh, is that not alright, Mrs Stapleton? Mrs Stapleton, why are you crying?' If it was me or any other of the nice middle-class kids we would have been strung up on the climbing frame and been beaten like a piñata.

Pause.

You always make excuses for shits like him. I bet you a million fucking pounds that he's got more praise postcards at home than anyone I know. And you probably fucking sent them.

AMANDA. It's the swearing that's bothering me most in this diatribe.

BECKY. I mean, we are seriously penalised just because we know what diatribe and piñata means. If I communicated with 'bare, sick and butterz' I'd have more awards than Judi Dench but because I'm white and middle class, it's just fucking assumed that I should have manners. That I should work hard, have aspirations to go to university, spend a gap year building irrigation systems in Mogadishu and know who Judi Dench is. It's so fucking unfair.

AMANDA. Where is Mogadishu?

BECKY. Dunno. I'll Google it later. The point is –

AMANDA. I think I get the point.

BECKY. Go to see Henderson tomorrow morning, yeah?

AMANDA. Mr Henderson.

BECKY. Tell him you were assaulted.

AMANDA. It's not that simple, Becky.

BECKY. God, it never is with you.

AMANDA's phone rings. She signals for BECKY *to stop talking as she answers.*

AMANDA. Hiya, love, fine... yep... okay... Can you get some coffee?... No, only instant crap left. Get the Douwe Egbert, yeah? The Colombian roast. Not the Brazilian, the Colombian... yeah...

BECKY (*shouting*). Mum was assaulted at work today.

AMANDA (*shut-up signs*). Just Becky being silly... Yeah. Got all the coursework in. Bloody miracle... *Mother* fucking *Courage*... I know. Yeah. What? (*To* BECKY.) What did you get in your physics exam?

BECKY. A-star.

AMANDA. She got an A-star.

Loads of whooping from the other end of the phone, AMANDA *pulls it away from her ear and laughs.*

I think he's pleased.

BECKY. Such a freak.

AMANDA. She said you're a freak. (*Laughs.*) Yeah, yeah, see you soon. (*She puts the phone down.*) That's great, Becky, well done, love. Shall we get a takeaway to celebrate?

BECKY. Are you going to tell Henderson?

AMANDA. How about an Indian? Or a Chinese? Fish and chips? Let's get fish and chips –

BECKY. You need to see him first thing.

AMANDA. Can we change the subject, please?

BECKY. He needs to be punished.

AMANDA. It's not all black and white. The world is not black and white. There's always grey.

BECKY (*groans*). Not the metaphors. I hate the metaphors.

AMANDA. I'm trying to explain.

BECKY. You break the law and you get punished. It's pretty standard the world over. He pushed you.

AMANDA. He was angry.

BECKY. And?

AMANDA. He was really angry.

BECKY. So what?

Pause.

Who was he fighting anyway?

AMANDA. A Turkish boy. Your year. Newish. Glasses. A bit, you know, nerdy.

BECKY. Not Firat. Please tell me it wasn't Firat. Did he have a briefcase?

AMANDA. Yeah, I think so.

BECKY. For fuck's sake, he's a friend of mine.

AMANDA. You've never mentioned him.

BECKY. He's not a friend-friend.

AMANDA. Oh, not a friend-friend.

BECKY. You know what I mean, not that kind of friend. I just know him.

AMANDA. So, he's not a friend.

BECKY. He's in my form. They take the piss out of him.

Pause.

AMANDA. Is he the one that sent you that card?

BECKY. No.

AMANDA. He is, isn't he?

BECKY. Shut up, it wasn't him.

AMANDA (*laughing*). That's hilarious.

BECKY. You're so immature.

AMANDA. Sorry.

BECKY. He's a fucking genius. He passed his maths GCSE when he was nine in Turkey. He did it as some correspondence thing.

AMANDA. Sounds like a catch.

BECKY (*ignoring her*). That arsehole Jason Chambers was beating up Firat Yilmaz and you're trying to protect him.

AMANDA. There are lots of things you don't know about Jason.

BECKY. Here we go.

AMANDA. It's true.

BECKY. What things?

AMANDA. You know I can't tell you.

BECKY. Then I guess I'll have to wait for his misery memoir – *A Child Called Shit*.

AMANDA. Becky, if you knew what I know, you'd think differently.

BECKY. But I don't, do I?

AMANDA. And statistically, if you're a working-class African-Caribbean boy, you are more likely to –

BECKY. Boo hoo, poor little black boy blah blah blah.

AMANDA. Some people have harder lives and –

BECKY. Loads of people have hard lives and they're not all wankers.

AMANDA. But –

BECKY. Let's face it, things haven't been easy for me.

AMANDA. I know.

BECKY. But do I burn hamsters or push teachers? No, because everyone has a choice, Mum, and Jason Chambers chose to push you because you're a soft touch and he knew it. I know it, Peter knows it and I bet Dad knew it too.

AMANDA (*she lifts her glass*). Game, set and match to Miss Rebecca know-it-all.

Scene Three

CHRIS*'s office.* CHRIS *is sitting.* AMANDA *stands in the doorway.*

AMANDA. I don't want to make a big deal.

CHRIS. Right.

AMANDA. I just thought you should know.

CHRIS. Right.

AMANDA. I stood in his way.

CHRIS. Okay.

AMANDA. I shouldn't have stood in his way.

CHRIS. Well...

AMANDA. Not in front of him. You know that with Jason, when he's like that, you shouldn't get in his way. I should have been more sensible.

CHRIS. Okay...

AMANDA. He wasn't really angry with me. He just lashed out.

CHRIS. You said.

AMANDA. I just thought I should tell you.

CHRIS. And you have.

AMANDA. I have.

CHRIS. Yes.

AMANDA. I mean, I thought about not telling you, because... but then I thought you should know, you know, in case... I don't know, I just thought you should know.

Pause.

And now you do.

Pause.

CHRIS. Mr Boudouani wanted Erkan Ali excluded for blowing up a crisp packet and popping it near him on the grounds of 'sensory violation', so you'll excuse me while I try to gather my bearings here and wonder if Pauline has spiked my coffee with MDMA and I have entered a parallel universe. Have I got this right? A student pushes you in front of a group of other students and you don't think this warrants an exclusion of any kind?

AMANDA. I know what it sounds like.

CHRIS. Amanda in bloody Wonderland.

AMANDA. But he's been doing so well.

CHRIS. And now he's bollocksed it up.

AMANDA. This will be a huge setback for him.

CHRIS. The others saw what he did.

AMANDA. What's to be gained from sending him home?

CHRIS. Let me think about that. Oh yes, the message that we don't tolerate violence in this school. For heaven's sake, don't be so –

AMANDA. I just worry –

CHRIS. Amanda.

AMANDA. I just worry what we're sending him home to.

CHRIS. That's not our problem.

AMANDA. It should be.

CHRIS. It's not.

AMANDA. But surely we –

CHRIS. We can't be everything. We're not social workers.

AMANDA. But if we think –

CHRIS. And we're not their parents. Christ, if we were, they'd be better behaved.

AMANDA. Please, don't do anything just to make an example of him.

CHRIS. It's probably on YouTube already, the little bastard.

AMANDA. What about if we meet, the three of us, he apologises, I accept and then it's done, sorted?

CHRIS. Write up what happened.

AMANDA. But –

CHRIS. As soon as you can.

AMANDA. But –

CHRIS. I'll take it from here.

AMANDA. What are you going to do?

CHRIS. You've told me. I'll deal with it. I'll add it to the bloody list.

Scene Four

Under the stairs. CHUGGS *and* SAIF *are smoking a spliff.*

CHUGGS. So we's outside Chickstop and she comes steaming over.

SAIF. Where was I?

CHUGGS. Mosque, innit.

SAIF. Is it?

CHUGGS. She goes, 'Whose dog is this?' And I go, 'What's it got to do with you?' And she gets this badge out and goes, 'I am an RSPCA inspector.' So I goes, 'It's my mum's.' She goes, 'What's it called?' And I go, 'Jackie Chan'. And she goes, 'What breed is it?' And I go, 'Japanese Akita Inu.' And she goes, 'That's a very expensive breed.' So I goes, 'What you tryin' to say?' And she goes, 'I'm just sayin' it's a very expensive breed.' And then Emmanuel comes out with Tyson who jumps up at her. And starts going proper mad at her. Like proper going at her, like it wants to kill her. And Emmanuel is laughin' and Tyson's got all this spit and shit round his mouth and every time Emmanuel pulls him back, he jumps back at her. And I'm tryin' to tell him that she the RSPCA lady. And she goes, 'He needs a muzzle.' And DeShaun goes, 'What about the dog?' And I crease, man. It was sick, man. And she gets that badge out again and shows Emmanuel and tells him she from the RSPCA and he needs to control his dog. And Tyson's still going for her. And Emmanuel shits himself and thinks the RSPCA lady will take Tyson if he don't control it so he gets this stick and starts hittin' him round the face. It was well bad. And she goes –

JASON *runs down the stairs.*

JASON. I need you to do something.

SAIF. Where you been, fam? Chuggs has built a fat one.

CHUGGS (*sings and gestures to himself*). Bob the Builder!

SAIF (*sings*). Can we smoke it?

CHUGGS (*sings*). Bob the Builder!

SAIF (*sings*). Yes we can!

They beatbox.

JASON. Shut up.

SAIF. What, bruv? What's the beef?

JASON. Henderson.

CHUGGS. What?

JASON. About yesterday.

CHUGGS. Oh yeah, when you battered Miss Phillips, innit.

SAIF. That was bad, man. She's safe. She a nice lady, Miss Phillips.

CHUGGS. She got a bare nice body as well for her age and that.

SAIF. Truth, innit. I cracked one off thinking on her.

JASON. Shut the fuck up.

SAIF. That is no way to get a favour, man.

CHUGGS. Yeah, how about a little sweet talk?

JASON. It's serious.

CHUGGS. What?

JASON. I need you to tell Henderson what happened.

CHUGGS. Is it?

JASON. You both need to say the same thing, you get me?

CHUGGS. We was here, innit.

JASON. You saw her run in, yeah? Where was you at the time?

SAIF. I was next to Chloe looking at her yum-yums.

CHUGGS. The imam ain't gonna like that.

SAIF. They's grown, eh?

CHUGGS. Maybe she got some chicken fillets. You know push 'em up, push 'em out.

SAIF. Chicken fuckin' fillets. Smoke and mirrors, man, smoke and fuckin' mirrors.

JASON. Where was you?

CHUGGS. Standing behind you. You trod on my foot, it fuckin' hurt. How much you weigh?

JASON. What?

CHUGGS. Just sayin' you need to lay off the Chickstop buckets for a while, you gettin' bacon, innit.

JASON. That Year Ten pussy was on the floor behind her. When she stood in front of me, you heard me say, 'Get out my way.'

SAIF. Yeah.

JASON. And she said, 'Leave him alone.'

SAIF. And you said something about him being a Paki.

JASON. And that's when she pushed me.

Pause. CHUGGS *and* SAIF *look at each other.*

CHUGGS. She never pushed you.

JASON. She pushed me, yeah?

CHUGGS *and* SAIF *look at each other.*

(*To* CHUGGS.) What?

CHUGGS. Nothin'. I just thought –

JASON. Henderson's gonna call you in, you get me?

Pause.

CHUGGS. Yeah.

JASON. It's important, yeah?

CHUGGS. Yeah, yeah. Safe. Cool. Whatever.

JASON (*to* SAIF). What about you?

SAIF. I dunno.

JASON. You was right by me.

CHUGGS. We was creasin' up, man, it was well funny. That boy trying to get away, he was shittin' himself, man.

SAIF. Jas, I dunno.

JASON. Fuckin' hell, the amount of trouble I got you out of back in the day.

SAIF. I know, man, but –

JASON. She pushed through, stood in front of me. I told her to move, yeah?

Pause.

Yeah?

SAIF. Yeah.

JASON. And she said, 'Leave him alone, you black bastard,' and pushed me, yeah?

SAIF *and* CHUGGS *look at each other.*

CHUGGS. Did she say that?

SAIF. Jas, man.

JASON. What?

CHUGGS. I never heard her say that.

SAIF. She never.

JASON. Just say it.

SAIF. We can't, man.

JASON. Just fuckin' say it.

SAIF. But she never –

JASON. You never saw her fuckin' push me so what does it fuckin' matter if you never heard her?

They look at each other.

She's a racist –

SAIF. But –

JASON. She said it quiet, right in my face. You saw her get right in my face, yeah?

CHUGGS. Do you remember when we was doing that book?

SAIF. She ain't like that.

CHUGGS. About the Boo Radley.

JASON. She was well angry.

CHUGGS. She said the word 'nigger' about a million times.

SAIF. She read it, you retard. It's in the book. Fuckin' hell, no wonder you have to have special lessons with the other spastics.

CHUGGS. Fuck you. She an idiot, man.

JASON. Yeah, man.

SAIF looks at him.

SAIF. She could get in bare serious shit for sayin' that.

JASON. I'm in serious shit.

SAIF. You can't just –

CHUGGS. She deserves it, man.

SAIF. What the fuck?

CHUGGS. I never liked her.

JASON. She deserves it, racist bitch. She lucky I didn't fuck her up.

DEE arrives, she puts her arms round JASON.

DEE. Who's lucky you didn't fuck her up?

CHUGGS. Miss Phillips.

JASON. She called me a black bastard.

DEE *laughs. Stops. Embarrassed. Not sure. There is silence.*

You heard her, yeah?

She lets go of him and looks at him. Pause.

DEE. Me?

JASON. You.

DEE. No.

JASON (*pointing at the other two*). They did.

They all look at her.

CHUGGS. She said it well quiet just before she pushed him.

DEE. What? It's jokes, yeah?

Silence. DEE *looks at* SAIF, *he shrugs.*

She didn't push you. You pushed her.

JASON. Why would I do that, Dee? For no reason? For no fuckin' reason at all?

DEE. Jas…

JASON. What?

DEE. You was angry.

JASON. Yeah, innit. I'll just tell Henderson that I was angry and everything will be just fuckin' forgotten.

Pause.

I just seen him, you get me?

Pause.

That bitch called me a black bastard. She pushed me and that's why I pushed her.

Pause.

Dee?

DEE. What?

JASON. I just told you what happened.

Pause.

Do you understand?

She looks at SAIF.

SAIF. Jas, allow it.

JASON. I'm talkin' to Dee.

Pause.

Dee? (*Soft.*) Dee?

He goes to her and kisses her, a gentle tender kiss.

Dee, I'm fucked.

She looks at him.

DEE. Yeah. Okay. Yeah.

Pause.

CHUGGS. What did you tell Henderson?

JASON. All of it, man. All of it.

Scene Five

CHRIS*'s office.* CHRIS *and* FIRAT.

FIRAT....and I was on the floor trying to pick my books up and unbreak my glasses.

He takes them off and shows them.

CHRIS. Yes, I know.

FIRAT. He broke them. Jason broke the glasses.

CHRIS. Yes, so when Miss Phillips –

FIRAT. Look, snap. My father asked me how this occurred and I tell him that I fell during hockey.

CHRIS. Firat –

FIRAT. He said, 'Why are you doing hockey? What about maths and science?' I try to tell him we must do everything but he doesn't believe me.

CHRIS. Yes, but what happened after Jason pushed you on the floor? When Miss Phillips came?

FIRAT. You know they should not be smoking in school. You know that.

CHRIS. Yes, I know that.

FIRAT. So why do you let them? They are always there, sometimes with class B cannabis. Everybody knows it. They do not attend the lessons –

CHRIS. When Miss Phillips separated you –

FIRAT. I never bumped him. He bumped me. He burnt his own shirt.

CHRIS. And she was standing in front of Jason –

FIRAT. He was shouting swear words at me. Very bad words. I do not want to say to you. Very rude.

CHRIS. You don't have to.

FIRAT. Racist slanderings, which is illegal in Britain, yes?

CHRIS. Yes, but did you see Miss Phillips push Jason?

FIRAT. I shall have him arrested. I do not want to say to you what he said. Very racist and rudist.

CHRIS. Firat, this is very important.

FIRAT. Arab cunt. Paki cunt.

CHRIS. Pardon?

FIRAT. What he said to me. It is terrible, is it not?

CHRIS. I see.

FIRAT. I am Turkish.

CHRIS. Did she push him?

FIRAT. Who?

CHRIS. Miss Phillips.

FIRAT. I didn't see.

CHRIS. Are you sure?

FIRAT. I didn't see.

CHRIS. Did you hear her say anything bad to Jason?

FIRAT. Bad?

CHRIS. Racist?

FIRAT. The teacher?

CHRIS. Yes.

FIRAT. I don't remember.

CHRIS. Nothing?

FIRAT. I heard her trying to stop. I tried to pick my books, unsnap the glasses. It was loud, very explosion.

CHRIS. You couldn't really say if she did or didn't, is that right?

FIRAT. Am I in trouble?

AMANDA *arrives*.

CHRIS. No.

Pause.

Hi, Miss Phillips, come in.

AMANDA. Sorry, I can come back later.

CHRIS. No, no, I think we've finished. Firat?

FIRAT. Yes, sir?

CHRIS. If you remember anything else, you must come to see me straight away.

FIRAT. Yes, sir.

He gets up.

AMANDA. Firat?

FIRAT. Yes, Miss?

AMANDA. Can you tell Becky I've got her maths book. She left it in the car.

FIRAT. Yes, Miss.

He goes. AMANDA *points at him and looks quizzical.*

CHRIS. Shut the door, Amanda.

AMANDA. What's going on?

CHRIS. Have you done the statement?

AMANDA. I've been teaching.

CHRIS. I need you to write it.

AMANDA. I'm free period four.

CHRIS. I'll get someone to cover you next period.

AMANDA. I can do it period four.

Pause.

CHRIS. There's been an allegation.

AMANDA. About Firat?

CHRIS. About you.

AMANDA. Me?

CHRIS. Yes.

AMANDA. Me?

CHRIS. You.

AMANDA. I don't understand.

CHRIS. Jason is alleging that you pushed him.

AMANDA. What?

CHRIS. Before he pushed you.

AMANDA. I didn't.

CHRIS. And that you said something.

AMANDA. What?

CHRIS. Did you?

AMANDA. I told him to stop.

CHRIS. Did you say anything else?

AMANDA. I don't think so.

CHRIS. You don't think so?

AMANDA. No, I didn't.

CHRIS. He's alleging that you racially abused him.

AMANDA. What?

CHRIS (*he finds a statement in the pile of papers and reads*).
    'Miss Phillips got really angry. She stood in front of me and...'

He hands her the paper.

She reads it.

AMANDA (*reading*). This is ridiculous.

She reads on.

I wouldn't say that.

She reads.

And I didn't touch him. Well, I did, but only to stop him
attacking Firat. How can you ask me? Christ, Chris.

CHRIS. I know, but I have to.

AMANDA. He pushed me.

CHRIS (*motioning to the statement*). He doesn't deny that.

AMANDA. I didn't provoke him. Other kids were there, they'll
    tell you.

CHRIS. I know.

AMANDA. Delilah Ogunleye was there, Jayden Haynes –

CHRIS. I know.

AMANDA. Chloe McGregor –

CHRIS. Amanda, I know. Jason's already told me.

Scene Six

Under the stairs. JORDON *is standing.* CHLOE *is looking at a magazine and sharing* DEE*'s headphones.* CHUGGS *is rolling a joint next to* SAIF*, whose eyes are shut.*

JORDON. Fuckin' hell, where is he?

DEE. He's comin'.

JORDON. I gotta go, man. What's the beef?

CHUGGS. He'll tell you when he gets here, innit.

SAIF. He'll be here in a minute, man. Calm down, innit.

   JORDON *is distracted by* CHLOE*'s magazine and grabs it.*

JORDON (*looks closer*). Why ain't she wearing knickers?

CHLOE. Publicity, innit.

JORDON. Publicity for her pussy?

CHLOE. No, for her career, innit.

JORDON. Is it? She bare fugly these days.

CHLOE. Butterz, innit. She mental. They lock her up in rehab.

JORDON. You don't get locked up in rehab. It ain't no prison. It's like a spa, but without the facials.

CHLOE. Is it?

JORDON. My auntie went. Robbie Williams was there the same time.

CHLOE. Is it?

CHUGGS. I hate that cunt.

JORDON. They all had to talk about their problems and shit and you ain't allowed to tell no one what is talked about cos it's all confidential and about the recovery, innit.

CHLOE. Is it?

JORDON. My auntie told me everything.

CHLOE. What she say?

JORDON. Some dark shit.

CHLOE. Is it?

JORDON. Some bare dark shit like stuff you can't even imagine in your worstest nightmares.

CHLOE. What sort of dark shit?

JORDON. Rotten nasty evil fuckin' bad dirty shit.

CHLOE. Like what?

JORDON. I can't tell you. It's confidential, innit.

CHLOE *turns the page*.

That's nasty, man. I like that dress, though, that'd be sick on you, Chloe, show off your titty titty bang bangs nice. Dee, what you think?

DEE. Yeah, it's nice.

JORDON. Look sex on Chloe, yeah?

CHLOE. Where's Jas?

CHUGGS. He's fuckin' comin'.

CHLOE. I gotta go.

JORDON. Shit, man, me too.

CHLOE. I need to munch. I gotta get pizza, I'm bare hungry, innit. Never had no breakfast cos my mum's a bitch.

JORDON. I gotta see Henderson.

SAIF *and* DEE *exchange glances*.

CHLOE. Why?

JORDON. A.M.

CHLOE. What?

JORDON. A.M. Academic Mentoring for those of us who is at risk of potential failure. Looks bad on them if we get Ds in the GCSEs. Looks good if we get Cs in the GCSEs, innit.

CHLOE. I wanna do that. That ain't fair, innit. Why do you get that?

JORDON. It's for potential failure, C/D borderlines. Not actual failure, like youse – F/G borderlines.

CHUGGS. Fuck you.

JORDON. None of youse qualify. 'Cept Dee. Dee goes to see Miss Frost, innit. But Dee's higher category – A/B borderline. She goes A.M.B.G.B.

CHLOE. What's that?

JORDON. Academic Mentoring for Black Girl Bodricks.

DEE. Fuck you.

JORDON. No, no, don't be shamed to be clever boots. Oh yeah, and Saif goes C.C.W.D.

SAIF. Whatever.

CHLOE. What's that?

JORDON. Curry Club for Wannabe Doctors.

Laughter.

SAIF. You're such a prick, man.

CHLOE. You missing maths?

DEE. I thought mentoring was after school, innit.

CHUGGS. After school? Waste, man.

DEE. It's only ten minutes.

CHUGGS. Is there food?

DEE. Jaffa Cakes.

CHLOE. Is it? I love Jaffa Cakes.

JORDON. Jaffa Cakes make your spunk taste of orange.

CHUGGS. Is it?

CHLOE. You's nasty, man.

DEE. Why ain't you seein' Henderson after school?

JORDON. I got a message to see him today, end of lunch. That headmaster can't get enough of me, innit.

DEE *and* SAIF *look at each other.*

CHLOE. I'm fuckin' starving.

JORDON. I hope Henderson's got Doritos.

CHLOE. You get Doritos? That ain't fair. I want Doritos.

JORDON. You better work harder at being a potential failure then.

CHLOE *tries to grab his bollocks.* JASON *arrives.*

SAIF. Jordon's gotta go see Henderson.

JASON. When?

JORDON. Now, innit.

JASON *looks at* CHUGGS *and* SAIF.

JASON (*to* SAIF). You?

SAIF. No.

JASON (*to* CHUGGS). You?

CHUGGS. Not yet.

He looks at DEE. *She shakes her head.*

CHLOE (*to* JASON). Did you know Jaffa Cakes make your cum orangey?

JASON. What?

CHLOE. Jaffa Cakes. Jordon says –

JASON. Shut the fuck up, Chloe.

CHLOE. What the fuck? Why you being rude for?

DEE. It's about that thing with Miss Phillips yesterday, innit.

JORDON. Is that why Henderson wants me?

JASON. Yeah.

JORDON. I never did nothin'.

CHLOE. No Doritos for you.

JORDON. Fuckin' hell. Why's it always me in the shit? It was you. It ain't fair. I never did nothin'.

JASON. She called me a black bastard.

JORDON. What?

CHLOE. Who?

CHUGGS. That bitch Miss Phillips.

CHLOE. Miss Phillips?

JASON. Yeah, Miss Phillips. She called me a black bastard. Just before she pushed me.

CHLOE. What?

CHUGGS. She did. I heard her as well, innit.

They look at him.

CHLOE. Why you lying for?

CHUGGS. It's truth – (*To* SAIF.) ain't it, fam?

They look at SAIF *who nods.*

(*To* DEE.) Ain't it?

DEE *half-nods and half-shrugs.*

CHLOE. She never –

JASON. She did.

JORDON. Oh, I get it.

CHLOE. She never said –

JORDON. She did, man. She did.

JASON. Let's go over it.

CHLOE. Why you's all saying –

JASON. Saif, you be me. Chuggs, you be that pussy from Year Ten and I'll be Miss Phillips.

JORDON (*to* CHLOE). Watch, man. Watch.

CHUGGS. Sick. I am sick at drama.

JORDON. Can I be Miss Phillips?

CHUGGS. No, your tits are too big.

JORDON. Allow it.

JASON (*to* SAIF). You're me, yeah?

SAIF. Get someone else to do it.

JORDON. I'll do it.

JASON (*to* SAIF). Just fuckin' do it.

SAIF. Alright, alright. (*Being* JASON.) I am angry. I am an angry brother. (*Goes up to* CHLOE.) Do you wanna fuck this angry brother, suck his angry dick?

She looks at DEE *and pushes him away. Laughter.*

JASON (*to* DEE). Where was you?

She looks at him.

Where was you?

DEE (*pointing*). Over there.

JASON. Where was you two?

CHLOE. What does it matter?

JASON. Stand where you was yesterday.

CHLOE. I don't remember, innit.

CHUGGS. You was next to Saif.

She goes and stands next to SAIF.

SAIF. Yeah, but I'm not being me. I'm being Jas.

CHLOE. So where was you?

SAIF. Over there. Jordon, you be me.

JORDON. Who's gonna be me?

CHLOE. I'll be you.

JORDON. But then who's gonna be you?

CHLOE. I'll go get Junique. She in the canteen. She can be me.

CHUGGS. Nah nah, don't get Junique.

JORDON. Shaniqua. Get Shaniqua.

CHUGGS. Yeah, man, get Shaniqua.

JASON. Just fuckin' stand somewhere near where you was yesterday.

They move into positions.

Right. Now tell him you burnt my top.

SAIF (*embarrassed*). You burnt my top.

CHUGGS *laughs*.

JASON. No, like you mean it.

SAIF (*exaggerating*). You burnt my top.

They laugh.

JASON. Fuckin' do it properly.

SAIF. Alright, I'm doing it. You burnt my fuckin' top.

JASON. You cunt.

SAIF. You cunt.

CHUGGS (*silly foreign accent*). I'm sorry.

They all laugh. DEE *puts in her headphones.*

JASON. You fuckin' prick, don't do it in a Paki voice, do it normal.

CHUGGS (*to* JASON). Alright, man. (*To* SAIF.) I'm sorry.

JASON (*to* DEE). What you doing?

DEE. What does it look like?

JASON. This is fuckin' important.

DEE. It's a waste of time. I'm going.

JASON (*holds on to her arm*). No, you're not. Just fuckin' stand there.

CHUGGS. Can we get on with it? I'm losing my character.

JASON. I mean it, Dee.

She leans against the wall.

Start from the beginning.

SAIF (*mutters*). For fuck's sake. (*Angrily.*) You burnt my top.

CHUGGS (*laughing*). I feel like a prick.

JORDON. He feels like a prick. Did you hear? He feels like a
prick. Batty.

JASON grabs hold of JORDON.

Alright, man. It's jokes, that's all, innit.

JASON lets go of him.

You need to get off the steroids, fam.

CHLOE. And the Red Bulls, innit.

JASON (*to* CHUGGS). Do it properly or fuck off.

CHUGGS. Alright man, I'll do it. (*To* SAIF.) It was an accident,
that's all.

SAIF. You burnt my fuckin' top.

CHUGGS. I'm sorry.

SAIF. Sorry ain't gonna get me a new top.

CHUGGS. What do you want me to do?

SAIF. Jump back in time and not burn a fuckin' hole in my
favourite fuckin' top, you get me?

CHUGGS. Don't be a silly billy.

They all laugh except JASON. DEE smiles.

That's what he said. (*To* SAIF.) Remember, that's why we
was laughing. (*To* JASON.) He told you to stop being a silly
billy, that's why we was laughing, innit? I'm just saying
what he said.

JASON looks at them all. They fall silent.

JASON. Start again.

SAIF. Fuckin' hell, allow it.

JASON *looks at him.*

JASON. Without the stupid words and the Paki voices.

CHLOE. What are we supposed to be doing?

JASON. Watch.

CHLOE. But we seen it yesterday.

JASON. Just fuckin' watch.

SAIF. You burnt my top, you fuckin' cunt, you burnt my fuckin' top.

CHUGGS. Sorry.

SAIF. You burnt my top.

CHUGGS. It was an accident.

SAIF. You burnt my fuckin' top.

CHUGGS. You bumped into me.

SAIF. This is my favourite fuckin' top.

CHUGGS. I said I'm sorry.

SAIF. Sorry ain't gonna get me a new top, is it?

CHUGGS. What do you want me to do?

SAIF. Go back in time and not to have burnt a fuckin' hole in my favourite fuckin' top, you get me?

CHUGGS. You shouldn't be smoking.

SAIF. Don't tell me what to do.

CHUGGS. But…

SAIF (*in his face, poking his chest*). I told you, don't fuckin' tell me what to do.

CHUGGS. Fuck off, you stupid pussy.

SAIF. Who you callin' stupid? You's fuckin' stupid.

CHUGGS. What?

SAIF. Everyone knows you's fuckin' stupid.

CHUGGS. Fuck you.

JASON (*shouting over the top*). Keep going.

BECKY *begins to walk down the stairs. On hearing the commotion, she turns to go the other way, but when she recognises* JASON *imitating her mother, she stops and listens to what is being said.* SAIF *has hold of* CHUGGS *by the shirt.*

SAIF (*in his face*). I will fuck you up. Watch. Watch.

JASON (*calling*). Boys, stop it.

CHUGGS. Get off me.

SAIF. You Arab cunt.

CHUGGS. Don't call me that.

SAIF (*furious*). What? An Arab cunt?

CHUGGS. Yeah.

SAIF. Alright, you Muslim cunt.

They are in each other's faces. The anger is real.

Why don't you just fuck off home, you stupid little prick?

CHUGGS. You think you's so fuckin' clever.

SAIF. Why don't you just go back to making bombs? You fuckin' piece of shit.

CHUGGS. Fuck you.

SAIF *violently pushes* CHUGGS *who falls on the floor. He gets up, goes to go for* SAIF.

JASON *gets between them.* SAIF *pushes* CHUGGS *again. He's on the floor.*

JASON. I said stop it. Now!

SAIF (*still going to get him*). Did you hear me? Fuck off, you Paki bastard.

JASON (*stands between them*). Leave him alone. I said leave him alone. Don't!

SAIF. Why? What you gonna do?

JASON. Stop it.

SAIF (*to* CHUGGS, *trying to get to him*). Fuck you, you piece of Paki shit.

JASON. That's enough.

SAIF. Fuck you.

SAIF *tries to get to* CHUGGS.

JASON. Leave him alone, leave him alone, you black bastard.

JASON *pushes him.*

SAIF *furiously pushes* JASON *on the floor in front of them all.* SAIF *goes to get at* JASON *again.* DEE *pulls him back.*

A beat.

Watching each other intently. Adrenalin. They look at one another, not sure of what has actually happened.

Pause.

Then JASON *begins to laugh,* CHUGGS *next, followed by* JORDON *and* CHLOE. *Screaming, hysterical laughter.* SAIF *looks uncertain and begins to laugh, followed by* DEE.

BECKY *moves away.*

Scene Seven

AMANDA*'s kitchen.* AMANDA *is marking coursework, big glass of wine and plate of spaghetti pushed to the side.* BECKY *is sitting on the countertop swinging her legs, twirling spaghetti in her fingers.* PETER *is at the table.*

BECKY. If he was here now, I'd punch him in the face.

PETER. Join the queue.

BECKY. And the rest of them. Actually, I think I might torture them.

PETER. Guantanamo style.

AMANDA *looks at* PETER.

BECKY. Tie them up.

PETER. Play Lady Gaga twenty-four-seven.

AMANDA. Don't encourage her.

BECKY. Tell them their families are dead.

AMANDA. Rebecca.

BECKY. Sexually humiliate them, film it, put it on YouTube.

AMANDA. That's not funny.

BECKY. I'd go for Chuggs first, he's a fucking moron, he'd probably enjoy it.

AMANDA. I get it, you're angry.

BECKY. They were laughing. They were laughing about it. About you.

AMANDA. They're children.

PETER. That's no excuse, little bastards.

BECKY. Big bastards.

    AMANDA *gets up and refills her glass.*

    They'll all lie. You know that, don't you?

AMANDA. They won't.

PETER. Amanda…

AMANDA. They won't.

    Long pause. They eat and drink. Silence. BECKY *stares at* AMANDA.

BECKY. What's the worst that could happen?

AMANDA. Can we get off this, please?

BECKY. If they do –

AMANDA. I was hoping for a relaxing start to the weekend.

BECKY. If they lie.

AMANDA. It's not going to happen.

BECKY. But if they do.

AMANDA *shrugs*.

You must have some idea.

AMANDA. Be disciplined, I suppose.

PETER. For assault?

BECKY. And racist abuse?

AMANDA. Are you trying to make me feel better or what?

BECKY. You don't know them.

AMANDA. I've taught all of them.

BECKY. That doesn't mean you know them. Fucking hell, Peter, tell her.

PETER. You've got to protect yourself.

AMANDA. They'll do the decent thing.

PETER. You sure about that?

BECKY. You always think everyone will do the decent thing.

AMANDA. They usually do.

BECKY. They don't. And they won't.

PETER. What did the rest of your department say?

AMANDA. Chris told me not to discuss it with anyone.

PETER. Did he?

AMANDA. He knows what he's doing, he's the head.

PETER. The acting head.

AMANDA. Yes, and he knows what he's doing.

PETER. I think you should contact your union.

AMANDA. I'll handle it my way.

PETER. But –

AMANDA. I don't want to go in all guns blazing.

BECKY. No, leave that to the black boys.

AMANDA. Becky.

BECKY. I'll kill him.

AMANDA. Stay out of this.

BECKY. Why should I?

AMANDA. It's got nothing to do with you.

PETER. Becky?

BECKY. What?

PETER. Your mum will sort it out.

Pause.

AMANDA. Are you listening?

BECKY. But they were laughing.

AMANDA. I'm a big girl. I can take care of myself.

BECKY. But –

AMANDA. It's all under control.

Scene Eight

SAIF *and* CHUGGS *are under the stairs, smoking.* SAIF *gets a Tupperware box out of his bag. Peels off the lid.*

CHUGGS. I hate Mondays. What's the point of Mondays? Why don't we start school on Tuesdays? What's those?

SAIF. Cakes, innit.

CHUGGS. Is it? Gimme one.

SAIF *takes out two fairy cakes from the box.* CHUGGS *looks carefully at the cake for a long time.*

Safe.

SAIF. My little sister made them.

CHUGGS. That is bare nice, man. Your little sister made us some little cakes with her little hands.

SAIF. They's not for us. For a cake sale at her school. For charity.

CHUGGS. Why you got them then?

SAIF. Rejects.

CHUGGS. Ahh, that's bare sad, poor little cakey rejects. (*To the cake.*) Come here, I feel your pain, I make it all better. (*He bites into it.*)

They sit for a long time eating cakes. CHUGGS *finishes his, smacks his lips and relights his joint.*

How did your little sister make them little cakes?

SAIF. Recipe, innit.

CHUGGS. Is it? Get it. Give it me.

SAIF. What for?

CHUGGS. I'm gonna make some.

SAIF looks at him for a second and bursts into laughter.

I like them. They's sick. I's a bare special cook. I could be a chef.

SAIF laughs. Stops laughing for a split second, looks at him.

Predicted a D in food tech.

SAIF erupts. CHUGGS *starts laughing.*

(*Laughing.*) Shut up, man. I could specialise in your sister's school charity cakes. I could be the next Gordon Ramsay. (*Impersonates Gordon Ramsay.*) These little fuckin' school cakes are fuckin' unber-fuckin'-lievable. If you fuckin' don't eat them, you are a fuckin' shaved cunt.

They crack up.

(*Laughing.*) You could work with me and be my kitchen bitch.

SAIF cracks up. DEE *walks down the stairs.*

SAIF. Alright, Dee? I can see your nipples through that shirt.

DEE. Why don't you stop looking at my tits and start reading your fuckin' holy book a bit more?

SAIF. Whoa, alright girl.

CHUGGS. Fuckin' hell, you got pre-mental tension or what?

DEE. What?

SAIF. It's premenstrual, you dick. He means premenstrual tension.

CHUGGS. Nah nah, in PSHE, Miss Levene was going on about pre-mental tension, how girls get pre-mental tension.

SAIF. Nah, she wasn't. She was saying menstrual. Premenstrual.

DEE. It's from the Latin 'mensis'. It means month.

CHUGGS. What's a month got to do with anything? And what's Latin?

DEE. It's an ancient language, innit.

CHUGGS. I never heard of it.

SAIF. It's like Shakespeare. Like the words in *Romeo and Juliet*, innit.

CHUGGS. That film is shit, man.

DEE. It's from before Shakespeare, Latin's from Roman times.

SAIF. Whatever. People don't talk it no more, innit.

CHUGGS. Like French. I fuckin' hate French. What's the point of French? Who talks French anyways?

SAIF. Miguel in 11F.

CHUGGS. He ain't French, he's black.

DEE. You can be black and French.

SAIF. He's from Chad, innit.

CHUGGS. Where's Chad?

SAIF. Africa, innit. Dee, is it?

DEE. Yeah.

CHUGGS. Why's he talk French if he's from Chad?

SAIF. It's what they talk there, I suppose.

CHUGGS. Why don't they talk Chadanese?

> DEE *starts laughing. She looks at* SAIF *who starts laughing.*

What? What's funny? If you live in Japan, you talk Japanese, innit. If you live in China, you talk Chinese, innit.

DEE. They talk Mandarin.

CHUGGS. What?

DEE. In China, they talk Mandarin.

CHUGGS. What the fuck's Mandarin?

SAIF. It's what they talk in China.

DEE. And it's a fruit.

SAIF. Is it?

CHUGGS. What the fuck's fruit got to do with anything?

DEE. It's like a satsuma. And you get Mandarin ducks as well.

SAIF. Like Peking duck, innit.

DEE. Peking duck is a recipe. I don't think it's a type of duck, not like a Mandarin.

SAIF. I thought it was a type of duck.

CHUGGS. What is all this shit about ducks?

DEE. No, it's probably where the recipe originates, Peking.

CHUGGS. What the fuck is Peking?

DEE. It's a place. Only now it's called Beijing.

CHUGGS. Where the fuck is Beijing?

DEE. It's in China.

CHUGGS. Where they talk Chinese. In China they talk Chinese. Like in Japan they talk Japanese. Every fucker knows that. So, if you live in Chad, you should talk Chadanese.

> *They laugh.*

SAIF. What do you talk if you live in England?

CHUGGS. English, obviously.

DEE and SAIF burst out laughing.

I don't know what you's laughing at. It's so fuckin' obvious. Gimme one of them little cakes. I don't know what's so fuckin' funny.

He takes the box from SAIF. He carefully selects one and offers the box to DEE.

Want one? Saif's little sister made them with her little hands.

DEE shakes her head.

DEE. No thanks.

SAIF selects another one. Silence. CHUGGS studies his cake hard.

SAIF just eats his.

I got to go see Henderson.

CHUGGS. Is it? He seen us already, innit.

DEE. What did he say?

CHUGGS. Just asked what we saw and that, if we heard stuff, innit.

DEE. Was she in there?

CHUGGS. Who?

SAIF. No.

Silence.

DEE. I'm going home.

SAIF. What?

DEE. I don't feel good.

SAIF. Go after you seen him.

DEE. I don't want to.

CHUGGS. Just see him, man, just tell him what happened.

DEE. Shall I? Go in and tell him exactly what happened. Chuggs, is that what I should do?

CHUGGS. I never meant that, innit. Tell him what Jas said.

SAIF. Dee, man, stop being so extra, just go tell him.

DEE. I can't, Saif.

CHUGGS. What the fuck are you on about?

DEE. She ain't done nothin' wrong.

SAIF. You have to.

DEE. If I go home, he'll just think I'm ill.

SAIF. He fuckin' won't, he'll know and then he'll call you in tomorrow or the day after or the day after until he gets your statement, innit.

CHUGGS. Yeah, man, just do it now, it ain't that bad. It's bare funny when you think about it.

DEE. It ain't funny, you idiot.

CHUGGS. Don't fuckin' call me a idiot, you mouthy bitch.

DEE. Fuck off. Leave me alone.

CHUGGS. No, I won't fuckin' leave you alone. Just do what you're told.

DEE. Don't tell me what to do.

CHUGGS. Sorry, forget my name ain't Jason Chambers, you only take orders from him, innit. 'Sit down, Dee.' 'Yes, massa.' 'Stand up, Dee.' 'Yes, massa.' 'Wipe my arse, Dee, and while you're at it suck my cock.' 'With pleasure, massa.'

DEE. Fuck this – (*Goes to leave.*)

SAIF. And what about Jason? He'll lose it when he finds out.

DEE. That ain't my problem.

CHUGGS. It fuckin' will be.

SAIF. If you don't go see him, we're fucked. Not just Jason, me and Chuggs as well. They'll know.

CHUGGS. Yeah, man, I'll get serious beats for this.

DEE. Good.

SAIF. My parents said they'll send me back home if I get in any more trouble.

CHUGGS. Wankers.

DEE. They always say that.

CHUGGS (*impersonating his mother*). Send you back to the village.

SAIF. They mean it this time. They got the air fare ready. I've seen it, they showed me. This is it. This is my last chance, innit.

DEE. Then why are you doing this?

Pause.

SAIF. For Jas, man, he needs us.

Scene Nine

CHRIS*'s office.* CHRIS *and* AMANDA.

AMANDA. What about Firat?

CHRIS. He doesn't know.

AMANDA. That's good, isn't it?

CHRIS. Five of them agree with Jason. One says he doesn't know. That is not good. Once an accusation like this gets momentum, the proverbial can really hit the fan.

Silence.

Amanda, we work under a lot of stress and I know that sometimes it can get too much. I understand that. Are you sure, absolutely sure that you –

AMANDA. Yes.

CHRIS. I wouldn't be doing my job if I –

AMANDA. I haven't done anything wrong.

CHRIS. Right. I know. I'm sorry.

AMANDA. He was the one being racist, he was calling Firat all sorts of racist names.

CHRIS. I know.

AMANDA. I mean really hideous things.

CHRIS. Yes, it's all in Jason's statement.

AMANDA. Is it?

CHRIS. He's got it all covered. He's covered every conceivable angle, the clever little bastard.

AMANDA. Has he?

CHRIS. We should have got rid of him a long time ago. We've tried every bloody thing: peer mentoring, teacher mentoring, basketball club, withdrawal, exclusion, inclusion, circus skills, days out to the bloody seaside. You know how hard it is to reach some of these kids and he is totally bloody unreachable. I said that to Mike, when I was Assistant Head, this boy is –

AMANDA. No one's unreachable.

CHRIS. You know what I see when I look at Jason Chambers? An interactive whiteboard. I see a brand-new sparkly interactive whiteboard. All the wasted time and money spent on supporting him, trying to make him a reasonable human being.

AMANDA. Come on, Chris.

CHRIS. Sue McCarthy's been asking for an interactive white-board in the drama studio for two years, I might give her Jason instead.

AMANDA. What about if I speak to him? If I just quietly –

CHRIS. That's not a good idea.

AMANDA. Explain how serious this is.

CHRIS. No.

AMANDA. But –

CHRIS. Jason's father is coming in later.

Pause.

AMANDA. Should I be here?

CHRIS. I'll handle it.

AMANDA. I think it would be good if –

CHRIS. I think you should go home.

AMANDA. I don't –

CHRIS. Take the rest of the day off. I'll get you covered.

AMANDA. I need to give my Year Elevens their coursework back.

CHRIS. Someone in your department can do it.

AMANDA. But I need to give them feedback.

CHRIS. You can do it tomorrow.

AMANDA. But –

CHRIS. Go and put your feet up.

AMANDA. I don't want to.

CHRIS. I'll see you tomorrow. Stop worrying. I said I'll handle it and I will.

AMANDA. Are you sure?

CHRIS. Yes, go home.

Scene Ten

FIRAT *and* BECKY *by the stairs*.

BECKY. It's all round school.

FIRAT. I know.

BECKY. Fucking liars. Tell Henderson that she didn't do it.

FIRAT. I cannot.

BECKY. Please.

FIRAT. I was on the floor.

BECKY. Please.

FIRAT. My glasses were on the floor. Cacophony. I could not hear anything, only shouting.

BECKY. But you do know she didn't.

FIRAT. I do not know your mother.

BECKY. But you know me.

FIRAT. Yes.

BECKY. Well then.

FIRAT. We are not our parents.

Pause.

BECKY. Just go and tell Henderson that you know she didn't push him and she didn't say it. It doesn't make any difference to you.

FIRAT. He has already spoke to me.

BECKY. But you could change your mind.

FIRAT. No.

BECKY. Say that you forgot but now you remember.

FIRAT. Post-tramautic stress.

BECKY. Yeah, something like that. Go and see him now.

FIRAT. I have double A-level mathematics.

BECKY. After.

FIRAT. I do not think I can do that.

BECKY. Please.

FIRAT. No.

BECKY. Look, all you have to do is say you've remembered.

FIRAT. I do not want to.

BECKY. What's the big deal?

FIRAT. I do not want to lie.

BECKY. My mum tried to help you.

FIRAT. I want no part of this.

BECKY. You fucking selfish arsehole.

FIRAT. Why must you swear? Why must everybody swear? My sister tells me a girl in her science class tells Mr Bektas to eff off. This girl is eleven years old.

BECKY. My mum was trying to protect you.

FIRAT. Yes.

BECKY. What do you mean, yes?

FIRAT. What do you want me to say?

BECKY. I want you to say that you'll help.

FIRAT. I cannot.

BECKY. But you could sort all this out. If you could just –

FIRAT. No, I am sorry. I do not want to have anything to do with it, with them.

BECKY. This is all your fault.

FIRAT. You think that because you have to blame. This is a normal very psychological response.

BECKY. Thank you, Freud.

Pause.

FIRAT. I don't know why they are like this.

BECKY. Because they're wankers who think they can do what they want.

FIRAT. Why do they think this way?

BECKY. Fuck knows.

FIRAT. Where are the parents?

BECKY. Stoned, prison, benefits office, social services, McDonald's.

FIRAT. Why don't they do anything?

BECKY. Like what?

FIRAT. Tell them they are bad. Take away their toys.

BECKY. Their toys?

FIRAT. The PlayStation, MP3, bicycle, mobile, the Wii.

BECKY. They don't listen to their parents.

FIRAT. Why not?

BECKY. Because they can't control them. No one can really control anyone else, not really.

FIRAT. I must disagree. In Turkey, you get whack if you do wrong.

BECKY. But what do they learn from that?

FIRAT. To follow the rules.

BECKY. That violence is normal.

FIRAT. Here violence is normal. In Turkey, students do not fight with their teachers. They should get whacked here in the school.

BECKY. Put it forward to year council. Who's our form representative?

FIRAT. Me.

BECKY *laughs*.

BECKY. Go for it, next meeting, see what they say.

FIRAT. They should get a grand big stick and beat all the bad ones.

BECKY. Put nails in it, do it in the playground for everyone to see.

FIRAT. I think maybe contravenes human rights.

She laughs. Pause.

BECKY. Do you like it here?

FIRAT. Yes.

BECKY. Have you got any friends?

FIRAT. You.

She laughs.

No jokes.

Pause.

You are not like the rest.

BECKY (*laughing*). Shut up.

FIRAT. You are kind.

She laughs and looks away.

Your mother will be okay.

BECKY. How do you know?

FIRAT. Because she has you.

Pause.

And your father, of course.

Silence.

Rebecca?

He touches her arm.

This is not your problem to solve this.

Silence.

Rebecca?

BECKY. My dad's dead.

Scene Eleven

CHRIS*'s office.* CHRIS, BEN *and* JASON.

CHRIS. How's Mr Grant's group?

JASON. Alright.

CHRIS. When do you meet?

JASON. Wednesday.

CHRIS. And how are you finding it?

Pause.

You know, has it given you space to…

Pause.

My understanding from Mr Grant is that it's to enable African-Caribbean boys to focus on achievement. Am I wrong?

Silence.

What do you do in the group?

JASON. Talk.

CHRIS. Good. Right. Okay.

Silence.

There is one thing I'm confused about in all of this. I wonder how did the other students hear Miss Phillips, if, as you say, she whispered it?

BEN. You've interviewed the other students.

CHRIS. Yes.

BEN. And?

CHRIS. They say what Jason said.

BEN. Why are you asking him then?

CHRIS. I've known Miss Phillips for a long time.

BEN. Are you suggesting that he's lying?

CHRIS. No, I'm not suggesting that.

BEN (*to* JASON). Are you?

JASON. No.

BEN. Are you lying?

JASON. No.

BEN. Are you?

JASON. No.

BEN. Are you sure?

JASON. Yes.

BEN. He's not. I'm telling you he's not.

Silence.

CHRIS. You've always got on well with Miss Phillips, haven't you?

Pause.

Jason?

JASON. What?

CHRIS. What do you think?

JASON. About what?

CHRIS. About what I just said.

JASON. Nothing.

CHRIS. Miss Phillips is a good teacher.

BEN. She's out of control.

CHRIS. Mr Chambers…

BEN. And she's racist.

JASON. She accused Chantelle of taking her purse when it was in her bag all along.

CHRIS. That doesn't make her racist.

BEN. Saying he's a black bastard does.

JASON. And in our English class she said black men were crap fathers. Crap fathers. That's what she said.

CHRIS. I can't speak for Miss Phillips, I don't know the context, but I'm sure there's an explanation for that.

BEN. And what explanation is there for her assaulting him?

CHRIS. I just want to make sure that Jason realises the consequences of an accusation like this. (*To* JASON.) Do you, Jason? Do you understand what could happen to Miss Phillips?

Pause.

Jason?

BEN. It's not his fault.

CHRIS. With respect, Mr Chambers, Jason did push her.

BEN. I make no apology for him standing up to a racist.

CHRIS. He was attacking another boy. And it's not the first time Jason's been in trouble for his aggressive behaviour. (*Shows a piece of paper.*) The behaviour contract that Jason signed during your last meeting with Mr Davies, which was – (*Reading.*) in May, I believe.

Pause.

I was going to exclude you. You know that, don't you?

BEN. He's not a mind-reader.

CHRIS. Miss Phillips didn't want me to. She told me what happened and she specifically asked me not to exclude you because she knew it was your last chance.

BEN. Why are you telling him this?

CHRIS. Jason knew that assaulting a teacher would get him permanently excluded.

JASON. I didn't.

BEN. He didn't.

CHRIS. And Miss Phillips was trying to protect you.

Pause.

Let me tell you what I think has happened here. You were fighting, Miss Phillips tried to stop it, you lashed out and pushed her and she fell on the floor. When you got home, you realised that you would be in serious trouble and you invented this to protect yourself.

Pause. BEN *looks at* JASON.

Jason?

Pause.

Is that what happened?

Pause.

Perhaps you might have made a mistake in your initial statement?

BEN. There's no mistake.

CHRIS. I don't want to lose a good teacher. I don't want the other students to miss out because of a lapse of judgement. Do you understand what I am saying to you?

Pause.

BEN. He's told you.

CHRIS. Mr Chambers, please.

BEN. The other students have told you.

CHRIS. It's not –

BEN. What has to happen to make you believe them?

CHRIS. I have to investigate.

BEN. No one supports her account. No one. Or have I got that wrong?

CHRIS. No.

BEN. Right, what happens next?

CHRIS. When we've investigated further then –

BEN. What else needs to be investigated?

CHRIS. I can't take action until –

BEN. Until what?

CHRIS. I'm trying to find out exactly what has happened here. I don't think you understand –

BEN. I'm assuming you've referred this to the LADO.

CHRIS. What?

BEN. The Local Authority Designated Officer –

CHRIS. I don't think –

BEN. In charge of abuse allegations.

CHRIS. It's all under control.

BEN. Isn't that the first thing that's supposed to happen?

CHRIS. I think we can solve this here.

BEN. I thought it was procedure to inform the local authority on the same day if a teacher assaults a child –

CHRIS. Allegedly assaults a child.

BEN. – as a matter of child protection. Or have I got that wrong?

CHRIS. No, you haven't.

BEN. So you've done the referral?

Pause.

You haven't done the referral.

CHRIS. I was hoping to –

BEN. And you've suspended Miss Phillips?

CHRIS. I can't discuss that with you.

BEN. But she should have been suspended when it's a matter of child protection.

CHRIS. Actually, that's not correct. If I think there's reasonable doubt –

BEN. 'Reasonable doubt'?

CHRIS. Yes, reas–

BEN. You've got six statements all saying the same thing.

CHRIS. Yes, but –

BEN. This is a joke.

CHRIS. I'm simply trying –

BEN. You think these kids can't be trusted and it's obvious why.

CHRIS. Mr Chambers…

BEN. You haven't done anything –

CHRIS. I can't just –

BEN. Because you want to pretend this hasn't happened.

CHRIS. I think –

BEN. You're responsible for my son while he's here. *Loco parentis*, Mr Henderson. And you've reneged on that responsibility. You haven't followed procedure because you thought you didn't have to.

CHRIS. With respect –

BEN. Because you thought you could just blame the black boy as usual.

CHRIS. No, that's –

BEN. I'd be interested to know what the Chair of Governors makes of all this.

CHRIS. I'm sure Paul Southgate will be –

BEN. And Miriam Harris.

CHRIS. What?

BEN. Miriam Harris, the Director of Children's Services. I take it you know who she is.

CHRI. Of course I know, but –

BEN. 'Embracing diversity, equality and excellence.'

CHRIS. What?

BEN. Your school motto.

CHRIS. What's that got –

BEN. It's an irony I'm sure most journalists would appreciate.

CHRIS. Now, just hold on. That's not helpful. You can't –

BEN. Don't tell what I can and can't do when you haven't even complied with your own school policy. I'm not sure you even know what the procedure is –

CHRIS. Of course I –

BEN. When you've been so unbelievably bloody negligent –

CHRIS. Mr Chambers, please, just –

BEN. No. My son has been assaulted. My son has been insulted. He's told you. Witnesses have told you. And now I'm telling you. I won't stand by and allow him to be treated like this. Do you understand? I will not allow it. Now, tell me, what action do you intend on taking?

Pause.

CHRIS. Miss Phillips has been suspended.

BEN. Is that right?

CHRIS. Yes.

BEN. For how long?

CHRIS. Indefinitely.

Scene Twelve

Under the stairs. JORDON, CHLOE, CHUGGS, SAIF *and* DEE. *All eating lunch.*

CHUGGS. I hate Mrs Scott, she's a bitch.

DEE. I think she's alright.

CHUGGS. Nah, nah, she's a control freak. Yeah, yeah, that's it, a control freak. The way she makes you do a stationery check and if you haven't got a fuckin' pencil, she goes mental. I mean, if I don't want to bring a fuckin' pencil then I don't have to, what's it got to do with her? You get me? What does she care?

SAIF. Maybe because you always borrow hers and it pisses her off.

CHUGGS. So what, man? I think the school should provide all that shit. I mean, they want you to have it, don't they? And when she talks, she always spits. It is ugly, man.

CHLOE. You's always chattin' about Mrs Scott.

CHUGGS. I'm tellin' you, she a nightmare.

JORDON. He wants to fuck her.

CHUGGS. That is rotten talk.

JORDON. Have you seen her toes in them skanky flip-flops? They's like Wotsits, man.

CHLOE. I love Wotsits. I haven't had Wotsits for time.

SAIF. He wants to suck her Wotsits, innit.

CHUGGS. Allow that.

CHLOE. She's fuckin' Mr Jones.

SAIF. Is it?

JORDON. But he batty.

CHLOE. Nah.

JORDON. How do you know?

CHLOE. Cos he's fuckin' Mrs Scott.

JORDON. No, I mean, how do you know that he fuckin' Mrs Scott?

CHLOE. Chantelle told me.

JORDON. Is it?

CHLOE. And her mum told her.

CHUGGS. Is it?

CHLOE. Cos she saw them.

SAIF. Is it?

CHLOE. In the alleyway behind The Swan.

ALL. Eurgh.

CHUGGS. What was they doing?

CHLOE. What do you think they was doing?

CHUGGS. That's nasty, man. And she a racist. Do you remember when she accused me of teafing her keys?

CHLOE. You did teaf her keys.

CHUGGS. I know, but she never knew that. She just picked on me because I got the biggest afro. Bitch.

They all laugh.

JORDON. What do you call two cannibals giving each other blowjobs?

SAIF. What?

JORDON. What do you call two cannibals giving each other blowjobs?

DEE. Gay.

JORDON. Nah, nah, other than gay.

CHUGGS. Batty.

JORDON. Nah, nah, other than that, it's a joke, innit.

CHUGGS. I don't get it.

JORDON. Cos I ain't finished it. What do you call two cannibals –

CHLOE. We don't know.

JORDON. You gotta say, 'We don't know, what do you call two cannibals giving each other blowjobs?'

CHUGGS. Why?

JORDON. It's what you say when you's told a joke, innit.

CHLOE. We don't know. What do you call two cannibals giving each other blowjobs?

JORDON. Nah, you emphasised the wrong bit, the wrong word. It's 'What do you call two cannibals giving each other blowjobs?'

CHLOE. What do you call –

JORDON. Nah, nah, not like that, like –

CHLOE. I don't fuckin' care what you call it.

SAIF. Why would two cannibals be giving each other
blowjobs?

CHUGGS. What's a cannibal?

DEE. It's a human who eats humans, innit.

CHUGGS. Why would a human eat a human?

SAIF. If they was hungry, I suppose.

CHLOE. And there weren't no other food.

JORDON. Yeah, but what do you call two cannibals givin' each
other blowjobs?

Pause.

Trust.

Pause.

Trust.

Silence.

Two cannibals givin' each other blowjobs. Trust, innit.

SAIF *starts laughing.*

CHLOE. That is disgusting. Jordon, you's a fuckin' disgusting
animal. Innit, Dee? He's nasty, ain't he?

DEE. Yeah, man. What is wrong with you? Where do you get
these things?

JORDON *bursts out laughing.* CHLOE *and* DEE *start
laughing.*

CHUGGS. I don't get it.

They all crack up. BECKY *comes down the stairs with*
FIRAT. CHUGGS *stands up.*

Oh yeah, come back for some more, have you?

FIRAT. No.

BECKY. I need to talk to you.

They look at her.

JORDON (*to the others*). Who dis?

CHUGGS. What is it, Goth girl? Spit it out.

BECKY. It's about my mum.

CHUGGS, SAIF and JORDON look bewildered.

FIRAT. Miss Phillips.

JORDON. Shit, man, no way, I never knew that.

Stands up, walks round her sizing her up.

Now you mention it, there is a family resemblance, particularly in the... (*Indicates her arse.*)

DEE. What do you want?

BECKY. To get this shit sorted out.

DEE. You should go.

JASON arrives. He puts his arm around DEE.

JASON. What shit?

BECKY ignores him and carries on. He is not used to this. They are unsure of how to react – they look from one to the other.

BECKY. She's never hit anyone in her life.

JASON. Why you giving me air for?

BECKY. Because you're a lying prick.

JASON. What did you call me? What did you fuckin' call me?

FIRAT. She did not mean it.

JASON. Mouthy bitch.

DEE. Jas.

FIRAT. She's worried about her mother.

JASON. That bitch is racist.

BECKY. That bitch has got a husband and he's black.

They look to see JASON's reaction.

JASON. You can still hate what you're fuckin'. (*Going up close to her.*) What about you? Are you like her? Is that why you's here? Have you come to be broken in? You know what they say about black men, don't you?

Laughter.

Do you want some black dick like Mummy?

BECKY. You don't scare me.

JASON. Don't I?

FIRAT. Please, leave her.

JASON. What are you? Her bodyguard? (*To* BECKY.) You might wanna choose a man rather than a boy.

BECKY. You might scare them, but you don't scare me.

CHUGGS. We ain't scared of him. What she chattin' about?

JORDON. Yeah, man, I ain't scared of no one.

DEE. She's chattin' shit.

CHLOE. Innit, you's chattin' shit.

DEE. It's time you went, girl.

CHLOE. Yeah, fuck off.

SAIF. Yeah, man. Why don't you piss off back to your cave?

High-fives. Sick.

FIRAT. Come, Rebecca.

BECKY (*to* JASON). Do you remember the school hall in primary?

JASON. What the fuck?

BECKY. Where we had assemblies.

JASON. No.

CHUGGS. Shut up and piss off.

BECKY. All the juniors sat on benches and the infants sat on the floor in front of them, you remember.

JASON. No, I don't, innit.

BECKY. When I was in Year Three, I always used to make sure I was sitting by the door so I could see everyone come in and I used to look for this boy, Tom Brewer. Do you remember him? He was in your year.

JASON. What the fuck are you chattin' about?

BECKY. I thought he was a wolf. Every assembly, I'd find him in with the juniors and watch him for clues. Even though he looked like a boy, I knew he was a wolf.

JASON. You're mental.

BECKY. I'm just saying.

JASON. What?

BECKY. I knew what he was. I knew exactly what he was.

JASON. You chat such shit.

BECKY. Just saying, that's all.

DEE *moves next to* JASON.

DEE. Take your boyfriend and your silly little stories and get the fuck away from here.

FIRAT. I'm not her –

DEE. We don't give a shit. Go.

BECKY. No one believes you.

JASON. Is it?

BECKY. They know what you're like. All of you.

DEE. And what are we like?

BECKY. Liars.

FIRAT. Rebecca.

CHLOE. Fuck you.

JASON. Henderson knows the truth.

BECKY. I know he does.

JASON. That's why he suspended her.

BECKY. Whatever.

JASON. She's at home now, innit.

BECKY. She isn't.

JASON. Henderson just told me. Call her.

BECKY. He wouldn't tell you that.

JASON. We had a meeting with him.

SAIF. It's true. Him and his dad.

JASON. And that's what he said. Call her.

CHUGGS. He got out science. Lucky bastard.

JASON. Ask her.

CHLOE. I know, man, it ain't fair. I hate science, innit.

JASON. Ask her.

BECKY. You're a liar. You're all liars.

　　BECKY *and* FIRAT *go. They watch them.* DEE *watches*
　　JASON.

JORDON. Fuckin' freaky gash.

SAIF. Quite fit, though. I would.

JORDON. Yeah, man. Fuckin' freaky fit gash.

　　DEE *puts her arms round* JASON.

CHUGGS. Was that boy really a wolf?

　　They laugh. FIRAT *appears again.*

JORDON. What?

CHUGGS. Fuckin' hell.

JASON. What?

FIRAT. I wanted to tell you –

DEE. What?

FIRAT. I have to tell you something.

CHLOE. Fuckin' hell, just say it, man.

FIRAT. Rebecca has no father.

JORDON. Join the club, man.

FIRAT. Her father is dead.

CHUGGS. Lucky bitch.

JORDON (*to* CHUGGS). Who is your daddy, anyways?

CHUGGS. Fuck you.

FIRAT. I do not think you understand.

JASON. So what, she ain't got no dad?

FIRAT. I thought it was important to know.

CHLOE. She got a stepdad, she just said.

FIRAT. He is not blood.

DEE. Who gives a shit?

FIRAT. But he is not her blood.

CHLOE. That's sweet, innit. He's protectin' her. That it is bare cute.

She goes up to him and puts her arms round him.

You is a cutey. (*Squeezing his cheek.*) Look at these cute little cheeks. I love these cute little cheeks.

FIRAT *shrugs her off.*

JASON. She can take care of herself. She don't need you.

FIRAT. But –

JASON. Stay out of it.

Scene Thirteen

AMANDA *and* PETER *in the kitchen. He has the phone in his hand and her union card.* AMANDA *has a bottle of wine open and exercise books out on the table.*

PETER. Bastards.

AMANDA. It's just for today. I'm going back tomorrow. Chris said –

PETER. Lying bastards.

AMANDA. If I knew you were going to come home, I wouldn't have phoned you.

PETER. Little lying bastards.

AMANDA. If I knew you were going to go completely over the top, I –

PETER. Little lying fucking bastards, I'll rip their fucking throats out – (*Speaking into phone.*) Hi, no sorry, I wasn't talking to you. No. Sorry –

AMANDA *starts laughing. He motions at her to shut up.*

(*To* AMANDA.) Shut up. (*Into phone.*) No, not you. Sorry. Yes. Sorry. Hello. The name's Amanda Phillips. No, not me.

AMANDA *laughs.*

She's my wife. Amanda Phillips, Amanda Phillips, Ms, that's right. (*Looking at the card.*) Her membership number is three-four-three-three-three-five-five. Yep. That's it. We need some legal advice. Thanks. I'll just pass you over to her.

He passes the phone to her. She takes it and hangs up.

What are you doing?

She takes the membership card and puts it back into her purse.

This isn't going to be sorted out by ignoring it. You need to do something. That's what you pay your union for. You've got to take control.

Pause. She smiles.

Why are you smiling like that?

Pause.

And why are you looking at me like that?

AMANDA. You're being everso caveman about this.

PETER *tuts*.

No, I like it.

PETER. It's not funny.

AMANDA. I know. It's very serious.

PETER. It is.

AMANDA. Yes.

PETER. Amanda, it is.

AMANDA. I think we should have some afternoon sex.

PETER. What?

AMANDA. I can't remember the last time we did that.

PETER. You need to speak to your union.

AMANDA. I love it when you talk official.

PETER. Amanda.

AMANDA (*goes to him*). Come here. We've got an afternoon to ourselves, let's –

PETER. You can't –

She starts kissing him.

What are you doing?

AMANDA. What do you want me to do?

He moves her away.

PETER. I want you to phone your union.

AMANDA goes to kiss him. He pushes her off.

What's got into you?

AMANDA. About half a bottle of Pinot Grigio and the scent of a potential shag.

PETER. Stop ignoring what's happening.

AMANDA pulls him to her.

Get off me.

AMANDA. You're making me feel like a sex-pest.

PETER. And stop drinking that. This isn't going to disappear. It's serious. Phone them.

AMANDA. There's no need. Chris'll sort it.

PETER. You've been sent home.

AMANDA. It's just for the day. I keep telling you, I'm home for the day. Chris said –

PETER. You need legal advice.

AMANDA. I just want to forget about it. I just want –

PETER. That boy, those kids are going to fuck everything up for you.

AMANDA. You sound like Becky.

PETER. She knows what they're like.

AMANDA. I know what they're like.

PETER. Really?

AMANDA. Why are you saying it like that?

PETER. Like what?

AMANDA. Like you think it's bollocks.

Pause.

PETER. You're too nice.

AMANDA. I'm not a pushover.

He shakes his head.

What?

PETER. You think that because you're supportive and kind to those kids, that they'll have your back. They won't. That sort only give a shit about themselves.

AMANDA. God, not this again. 'That sort' –

PETER. Some people are arseholes and always will be.

AMANDA. Jason isn't an arsehole. He's a boy with –

PETER. Don't say 'issues'. Please don't say 'issues'. I will have to divorce you if you say 'issues'.

AMANDA. Problems, then. And don't say 'everyone has problems'.

PETER. Everyone has problems. He needs a good slap.

AMANDA. Yes, Peter, that's exactly what he needs.

PETER. Some fucking discipline.

AMANDA. And you know just the man for the job, I suppose. Is he five foot ten and African-Caribbean by any chance?

PETER. You're allowed to say 'black', you know.

AMANDA. Why are you being such a prick?

PETER. Because you're so… sometimes you're just so fucking –

AMANDA. What? What am I?

PETER. That boy doesn't give a shit about you.

AMANDA. Can we talk about something else?

PETER. That boy doesn't give a shit about anyone.

AMANDA. If you're not going to have sex with me – (*Picking up a pen.*) I'm going to get on with this.

PETER. Thinking he's got away with it.

AMANDA. He won't –

PETER. Little bastard.

AMANDA. He's not –

PETER. Piece of shit.

AMANDA. You don't know him.

PETER. I know his type.

AMANDA. Why do you always revert to this inflexible position? Why can't you try to understand?

PETER. You think you understand? You think you know what's going on in that boy's head?

AMANDA. He's scared.

PETER. No one has to be a fuck-up.

AMANDA. I know, but –

PETER. A boy like him doesn't have to be a fuck-up.

AMANDA. There's pressures on him that you –

PETER. When I was fifteen –

AMANDA. We're not talking about you. It's different –

PETER. Here we go.

AMANDA. With gangs and –

PETER. There's always been gangs, but they were white, wearing fourteen holes and chasing me and every other coon they saw.

Silence.

He doesn't deserve your sympathy.

Pause.

AMANDA. I can't help how I feel.

PETER. He doesn't deserve it.

AMANDA. I can't help it. He's –

PETER. Stop making excuses for him.

AMANDA. I'm not, I'm trying to –

PETER. You'll lose your job and then what? What about Becky? What about the mortgage? What about us? You're willing to put it all at stake for a boy you hardly know, a boy who doesn't give a shit, for a group of kids who don't give a fuck who they hurt.

AMANDA. They're not like that. He's not like that –

PETER. Of course he's like that. For fuck's sake, wake up, Amanda, he's played you, they all have, and you haven't got a clue. It would be funny, if it wasn't so pathetic.

The door slams. BECKY *comes in and dumps her school bag on the table.*

BECKY. Why didn't you tell me?

AMANDA. Why are you here?

BECKY. I've been ringing you.

AMANDA. Have you bunked off?

BECKY. I've been ringing you all afternoon.

AMANDA. What for?

BECKY. Don't pretend you don't know. Don't fucking pretend.

PETER. Calm down.

BECKY. What's it got to do with you?

AMANDA. Becky!

BECKY. Why am I always the last to know anything around here?

PETER. We don't know what you're talking about.

BECKY. About her.

AMANDA. What about me?

BECKY. Being suspended. You being suspended.

AMANDA. Chris sent me home.

BECKY. I know.

AMANDA. For the day.

PETER. It's just for today.

AMANDA. He hasn't suspended me.

BECKY. That's not what Jason said.

PETER. What?

AMANDA. I told you to keep away from him.

PETER. How would he know?

AMANDA. I specifically said to keep out of this.

BECKY. Henderson told him.

AMANDA. It's not true.

BECKY. Why would he say it?

AMANDA. I don't know.

BECKY. His dad was there too.

Pause. AMANDA *picks up her phone*

They had a meeting this afternoon.

AMANDA. How do you know?

BECKY. Jason told me.

AMANDA *dials*.

I just fucking said. Henderson told them both at the meeting. He said he's suspended you.

Pause.

AMANDA. Hi, Pauline, it's Amanda. Amanda Phillips. Hi. Is Chris available?

End of Act One.

ACT TWO

Scene Fourteen

BEN's *house*. JASON *and* BEN *at the table*. BEN *eats*.

JASON. That was sick the way you laid into him. The way you told him what you thought and how you wasn't gonna take it. And when you said about procedure and that, he was scared, he didn't know what to say. He just kept repeating himself – 'We have to investigate it further.' And you wouldn't let him off the hook. You wouldn't let him get away with it. He was sweatin', man. Did you see? He was sweatin'. And when you said about the school motto and the newspapers and that, that was like a killer blow. He was well scared. Didn't you think? And when you said, 'my son' I was proud, innit. Yeah, I was well proud that you was my dad. I mean, it was like you was on fire, chattin' about procedure and that. You KO'd him. He must know that he can't get out of it. That she can't get out of it. Now that you're on it. There is no escape. Man, there is no escape.When you said –

BEN *slams his fist down*. JASON *stops immediately. Silence*. BEN *eats. Silence*.

BEN. Is that your school shirt?

Pause.

Why haven't you changed?

Pause.

Why haven't you changed your shirt?

JASON. I forgot.

BEN. How many times do you have to be told?

JASON. I forgot.

BEN. I heard you.

JASON. Sorry.

BEN. How many times?

Pause.

When are you going to start listening?

JASON. I'll change it now.

He gets up.

BEN. Sit down.

JASON. I'll just –

BEN. Sit down.

Silence.

You thought that was good today, did you?

JASON *nods.*

Really showed him, didn't I?

Pause.

Didn't I?

JASON. Yeah.

BEN. Yes.

JASON. Yes.

Pause.

BEN. Is that what you think?

JASON. I was proud of you.

BEN. Were you?

Silence.

JASON. I haven't done anything wrong.

BEN. You should have that printed on a T-shirt.

JASON. I didn't do anything.

BEN. And that.

Silence.

What's the colour of the carpet in that office?

JASON. What?

BEN. The carpet, in the head teacher's office, what colour is it?

JASON. I don't know.

BEN. Think about it.

Pause.

JASON. Blue.

BEN. What shade?

JASON. What?

BEN. What shade of blue?

JASON. I don't know.

BEN. Light or dark?

JASON. Dark.

BEN. How many kids at your school know that?

JASON. I don't know.

BEN. How many do you think?

JASON. I don't know.

Silence.

BEN. I bet there are some parents who've never even been in that office.

Pause.

Are there?

JASON. I don't know.

BEN. No, I don't suppose you do.

Silence.

Do you want to end up like me?

JASON. There's nothing wrong with you.

Pause.

You've done good.

BEN. You think this is good?

JASON. We're alright.

BEN. Look around you, boy. This is not good.

Pause.

Is it?

JASON. I don't know.

Pause.

BEN. If they exclude you –

JASON. She pushed me. She did. She –

BEN. If they permanently exclude you, it's all over.

JASON. She pushed me and then she said –

BEN. What do you think is going to happen?

JASON. She did –

BEN. What will happen to you if they kick you out?

JASON. I don't know.

Pause.

BEN. I keep telling you. I tell you to keep out of trouble. And you don't. I tell you to do your work. And you don't. I tell you to be respectful to your teachers. And you're not. I tell you to choose your mates carefully. And you don't. I tell you to speak properly and you don't. It's not that you can't. It's that you won't. You won't do it. You have no respect for anybody. You have no respect for me or –

JASON. I do.

BEN. Don't fucking interrupt me.

Pause.

I've been telling you for the last seven years to get out of your school uniform when you come home. It's so simple, an idiot could do it. It's so unbelievably simple and yet you don't seem to be able to manage it.

Pause.

JASON. Sorry.

Pause.

BEN. Do you know who you remind me of when you say sorry?

Pause.

Do you?

Pause.

JASON. Yes.

BEN. Who?

JASON. Mum.

BEN. And what do you think she would say about all of this?

JASON. I don't know.

Pause.

BEN. I'm going to give you one more chance to tell the truth. So think very carefully about what you say.

JASON. I'm telling –

BEN. Think about it.

Silence. BEN *nods at him.*

JASON. It's all true.

BEN. If I find out you're lying to me.

JASON. I'm not.

BEN. I gave him my word, do you understand?

JASON. Yes.

BEN. No, I don't think you do, boy.

JASON. I do.

    Pause.

    I understand. I swear –

    BEN *puts his hand over* JASON*'s mouth.*

BEN. My word. I gave him my word.

Scene Fifteen

CHRIS*'s office.* AMANDA *and* CHRIS.

CHRIS. I thought I could defuse it. I tried to persuade him. I tried. I did. Now I've got Miriam bloody Harris's flunkies chewing my ear off.

AMANDA. Who?

CHRIS. Children's Services. Wanting to know, no, demanding to know, why I didn't make the referral earlier.

AMANDA. What does that mean?

CHRIS. It's ridiculous.

AMANDA. What does that mean for me?

CHRIS. They're saying I should have referred the allegation straight away. That I shouldn't have seen Mr Fuckface Chambers first, which is totally fucking ludicrous –

AMANDA. What's going to happen?

CHRIS. They're living in cloud-cuckoo-land if they think any head teacher –

AMANDA. Chris –

CHRIS. I don't know yet, once the investigation is over –

AMANDA. How long will that take?

CHRIS. I don't know.

AMANDA. What do you mean? What I am supposed to –

CHRIS. Can I ask you something?

AMANDA. What?

CHRIS. When you came in, you said you weren't going to tell me –

AMANDA. Yeah.

CHRIS. Why weren't you going to tell me?

AMANDA. You know why. When can I come back?

CHRIS. When we've had the case conference, I'll –

AMANDA. What case conference?

CHRIS. There's a case conference, a strategy-meeting thing.

AMANDA. I don't understand.

CHRIS. It's a multi-agency thing to discuss the allegation.

AMANDA. What does that mean?

CHRIS. When a CP referral is made, everyone has to get together.

AMANDA. Who's everyone?

CHRIS. You know, the local authority representative, social services, the police...

AMANDA. What?

CHRIS. It's just to compare notes –

AMANDA. What for?

CHRIS. To make sure you're not a risk.

AMANDA. To who?

CHRIS. Children.

AMANDA. I don't believe this.

CHRIS. It's child-protection procedure.

AMANDA. I don't bloody believe this.

CHRIS. I'll give my opinion on the situation and then a decision is made about whether further investigation is needed, what the next step should be –

AMANDA. And who makes the decision?

CHRIS. Everybody.

AMANDA. They don't know me.

CHRIS. It's about sharing information.

AMANDA. What information?

CHRIS. If there's been previous allegations, that sort of thing. If you're already known to the police or social services.

AMANDA. Christ...

CHRIS. You've nothing to worry about. You've done nothing wrong.

AMANDA. Then why have you suspended me?

CHRIS. Suspension is a neutral act; it's not a disciplinary action.

AMANDA. Chris.

Pause.

CHRIS. We have to be seen to be accountable.

AMANDA. Seen?

CHRIS. We have to be accountable. We have to be seen to be doing something.

AMANDA. We?

CHRIS. Amanda.

AMANDA. It's you. You're in charge.

CHRIS. God, if only that were true.

AMANDA. This is ridiculous.

CHRIS. Welcome to my world.

Silence.

AMANDA. When is it?

CHRIS. Ten thirty.

AMANDA. Today?

CHRIS. Yes.

AMANDA. Where?

CHRIS. You can't be there. You're not allowed.

Pause.

AMANDA. It's everyone against me.

CHRIS. It's not like that.

AMANDA. It's exactly like that.

CHRIS. I know that it must feel –

AMANDA. You've no idea.

CHRIS. I'm sorry if this feels disloyal to you, but it's the way it is. Every allegation must be taken seriously.

AMANDA. Even when you know it's bollocks.

CHRIS. Yes.

AMANDA. I've spoken to my union. I've got an appointment to see the borough representative.

CHRIS. I think that's wise.

AMANDA. Do you?

CHRIS. Yes, you need someone official on your side, to represent –

AMANDA. I thought you were on my side.

CHRIS. I am. I just meant... I am on your side.

Scene Sixteen

Under the stairs. JASON, CHLOE, SAIF *and* CHUGGS.

SAIF. The feds?

JASON. Yeah, fam.

CHLOE. You went to the feds?

JASON. Innit.

CHLOE. Yesterday? When you wasn't here? You was with the feds?

JASON. Yeah. You should have seen my dad, man –

SAIF. What did they say?

JASON. They's gonna call her in.

CHUGGS. Shit.

CHLOE. Shit.

SAIF. Shit, man.

JASON. That bitch is gonna get it.

CHUGGS. Is it?

CHLOE. Shit.

SAIF. Shit.

JASON. They's gonna investigate.

ALL. Shit.

JASON. Then they's gonna charge her.

> *Pause.*

With assault and racist abuse. It's a hate crime.

> *Pause.*

She'll go to court.

> *Pause.*

My dad says we got to stand up for ourselves, innit.

> *Pause.*

It's truth, innit.

> *Pause.*

You all have to go to the station, yeah?

CHLOE. What?

JASON. You got my back, yeah?

SAIF. Why do we have to go to the feds?

JASON. Give witness statements, innit.

SAIF. Did they say that?

CHUGGS. It ain't like that. You don't just walk in and –

JASON. Looks better if you volunteer, yeah? Without being called, you get me?

SAIF. I don't think they'll listen to us.

JASON. Shows you go the extra mile, innit.

CHLOE. When my brother was –

JASON. Shows you's on my side, yeah?

Pause.

SAIF. Jas, the feds, that's a bit –

JASON. A bit what?

CHLOE. Extra.

SAIF. Yeah, man, it's a bit extra.

JASON. What the fuck you chattin' about? It's nothin'.

CHLOE. It ain't nothin'.

JASON. Go in, say you want to make a statement and tell them what you saw, innit.

SAIF. It's one thing tellin' Henderson, but tellin'–

CHUGGS. I'll do it.

SAIF *and* CHLOE *look at him.*

Fuckin' hell, I know most of them pigs anyway. They's practically family.

JASON *looks at* SAIF *and* CHLOE.

SAIF. But it ain't like Henderson. (*To* CHUGGS.) You could get in serious shit, man. Think about it.

JASON. What the fuck you doing?

SAIF. I'm just tellin' him.

JASON. It's his fuckin' decision.

CHUGGS. Yeah, it's my fuckin' decision.

JASON. He can do what he wants. You ain't his dad.

SAIF. Jas, come on. It's Chuggs, man, allow it.

CHUGGS. What the fuck?

JASON. What the fuck does that mean?

CHUGGS. What you fuckin' chattin' about?

SAIF. Forget it.

CHUGGS. Nah nah, go on.

SAIF. Nothin', man. It's cool.

CHUGGS. Nah, I wanna know what you mean.

CHLOE. He didn't mean nothin'.

CHUGGS. What the fuck's it gotta do with you?

CHLOE. Fuck you.

SAIF. You need to think it through, fam.

CHUGGS. What, cos I'm so thick I can't make my own decisions? Cos I have to have lessons with the other spastics? Is that what you's saying?

SAIF. Allow it, man.

CHUGGS. You can go fuck yourself. You always think you's better than me. You's always takin' the piss. You's think I don't know, cos you think I'm so fuckin' thick. Well, I ain't.

SAIF. I don't think –

CHUGGS (*to* JASON). Look at him, he's shook. (*To* SAIF.) You's always been like this, a pussy.

SAIF. We could all get in serious shit. Come on, Jas, tell him, man.

JASON. Tell him what? Tell him not to have my back.

SAIF (*going up to* CHUGGS). Chuggs, listen, man –

JASON (*pulling him away*). What the fuck are you doing? Leave him. You heard what he said. You heard him. He's right. You's a pussy, man. You's a fuckin' pussy.

SAIF *goes to walk away.*

Don't fuckin' walk. (*Pulling him back.*) You listen, yeah, I have had your back for time, man. I stuck up for you when they was all after you, remember? I been there for you, fam. I have always fuckin' been there for you, you get me? If it was you, I'd do it. If it was you, I'd do what I could, no question.

SAIF. Jas, man, I can't. My mum and dad, when they find out the truth…

JASON. No one's gonna find out. We all say the same thing. No one's gonna find out. If we all say the same thing.

SAIF. I ain't doing it.

SAIF *walks away.*

JASON. Where you going? What you doing? I'll fuck you up. Watch. Watch, man. You's either with me or… I'm tellin' you. Watch.

SAIF *goes.*

CHLOE. I've gotta go, man, it's science. Jarvis goes mental if you's late.

JASON. Chloe.

CHLOE. Yeah.

JASON. I need you to do this.

He goes up to her. Close.

It's bare serious now.

She looks up at him.

Can you do it?

Pause.

CHUGGS. Just say 'yes', you silly bitch.

CHLOE. Fuck you.

JASON. Chuggs, man.

CHUGGS. What?

JASON. I'm chattin' to Chloe.

CHUGGS. Sorry, man.

JASON. I wouldn't ask if it weren't important.

CHLOE. I know.

JASON. I wouldn't want to put you in that position.

CHLOE. I know.

Pause.

JASON. I like you.

Pause.

Have a think, yeah?

CHLOE. Okay.

JASON. You don't have to make up your mind now, innit.

Pause.

CHLOE. I'll go with Chuggs. We'll go together.

JASON kisses her. She goes. CHUGGS watches.

CHUGGS. You got all the hens, innit.

JORDON arrives.

JORDON. Where's Chloe?

CHUGGS. She's gone science.

JORDON. I got her phone. That sketty ho Mrs Horowitz took it off of her so I teafed it out her bag when she wasn't lookin'. 'You gotta pick a pocket or two.' You remember that in primary? I was Fagin. Chuggs, you was a flower seller.

Silence.

Was the matter? Who died?

They look at him.

Oh my days, has someone actually died?

They look at him.

No one has died, innit.

JASON. You gotta go police station laters.

JORDON. What for?

JASON. I'm pressing charges against Miss Phillips.

JORDON. For why?

JASON. Why do you fuckin' think?

CHUGGS. The assault.

JASON. You gotta go and ask to give a statement.

JORDON. I gotta pick my little sister up.

JASON. Go after.

JORDON. I gotta get her something to eat, innit.

JASON. Go after.

JORDON. My mum's not back from work till ten.

JASON. Fuckin' take her with you then. This is fuckin' serious,
    fam.

    Pause.

JORDON. Who else is going?

JASON. Chuggs.

    JORDON *laughs.*

CHUGGS. What the fuck? What you laughing for?

JORDON. Nothin', bro. Nothin'. Just –

CHUGGS. Just what? What? Fuckin' what? Fuck.

JORDON. You's can be a little eager, that's all I is saying.

CHUGGS. Eager?

JORDON. Like a puppy dog.

CHUGGS. What the fuck you chattin' about? I ain't no dog.

JORDON. Forget it.

CHUGGS. I ain't no one's bitch.

JORDON. Forget it, man. Forget it.

Pause.

Is Chloe going?

JASON. Yeah.

JORDON. Is it?

JASON. Yeah.

JORDON. Alright, man.

JASON. Cool.

JORDON. I have to take my sister, though, and she gonna want sweets. I's tellin' you, that girl cannot keep her mouth shut unless it full of flying saucers and Sherbert Dib Dabs.

SAIF *comes back.*

Alright, man?

SAIF. Alright.

JORDON. You stepped in dogshit or what?

Pause.

What's the butterz face for?

Silence.

Shit, what is this atmosphere? I can smell da doom.

JASON (*to* CHUGGS). I see you later, yeah?

CHUGGS. Yeah, man. (*To* JORDON.) They got business.

JORDON. Is it?

CHUGGS. Yeah, man.

JORDON. I gotta give Chloe her phone anyways.

CHUGGS. Laters.

They go. SAIF *and* JASON *sit alone. Silence. A long time.*

SAIF. I'll do it.

JASON *nods.*

Scene Seventeen

BECKY *is in the kitchen sitting at the table. She has a small box of raisins. She is lining them up in a row.* AMANDA *and* PETER *come in.*

BECKY. What happened?

AMANDA. Why aren't you at school?

BECKY. Came home.

AMANDA. I told you to stay at –

BECKY. What happened?

    PETER *puts the kettle on.* AMANDA *sits at the table.*

    Well?

PETER. Give your mum a moment.

BECKY. What did they say?

PETER. Becky.

BECKY. Well?

AMANDA. In a minute, love.

BECKY. I've been waiting here for two hours so stop treating me like a fucking kid.

PETER. That's enough.

BECKY. Am I talking to you?

AMANDA. Don't speak to Peter like that. Apologise.

BECKY. Yeah, alright, sorry, whatever.

AMANDA. Properly.

BECKY. Sorry.

AMANDA. My head's killing me.

PETER. I'll get you a paracetemol.

AMANDA. There's none left. (*To* BECKY.) Have you got any in your room?

BECKY. Why would I?

PETER. I'll look.

BECKY. Don't go in my fucking room.

AMANDA (*to* BECKY). Stop it.

PETER. I'll go to the shop.

AMANDA. You don't have to.

PETER. We need some more anyway.

Pause.

You'll be alright, yeah?

He kisses her.

BECKY. I'll look after her.

PETER (*to* BECKY). Do you want anything?

BECKY. No.

He goes.

AMANDA. I don't like it when you're rude to him.

BECKY. I don't want him going in my room.

AMANDA. You're being ridiculous.

BECKY. He's got no right.

AMANDA. Since when?

BECKY. Since you and him started sneaking around.

AMANDA. What?

BECKY. Not telling me anything.

AMANDA. We've only just got in.

BECKY. I have a right to know what's going on, don't I?

AMANDA. Not when you stamp your foot like a spoilt brat.

Pause.

BECKY. What did they say?

Pause.

AMANDA. The policewoman said I didn't seem very sorry.

BECKY. What did you say?

AMANDA. Nothing.

BECKY. Why didn't you tell her you had nothing to be sorry for?

AMANDA. My solicitor advised me to say nothing.

BECKY. Why didn't you stand up for yourself?

AMANDA. I just told you.

BECKY. What else did they say?

AMANDA. They asked me what happened.

BECKY. And what did you say?

AMANDA. I told them.

BECKY. And what now?

AMANDA. They're investigating.

BECKY. What does that mean?

AMANDA. It means they think Jason is telling the truth.

Pause.

They had a photograph of his chest.

BECKY. What?

AMANDA. He had these marks on his chest, like bruises.

BECKY. I don't understand.

AMANDA. Like someone had punched him.

BECKY. How did he get them?

AMANDA. From me, supposedly.

BECKY. That fucking snake.

AMANDA. How do you think he got those bruises?

BECKY. I dunno, he probably got Chuggs or Saif or one of those pricks to do them.

AMANDA. I can't stop thinking about it.

BECKY. Forget the bruises.

AMANDA. Who would do that to him?

BECKY. Forget him. What about you?

Pause.

Mum!

AMANDA. What?

BECKY. For fuck's sake.

AMANDA. Becky, you're not helping.

Silence.

BECKY. I wish Dad was here.

Pause.

This wouldn't be happening if he was.

Pause.

Would it?

Pause.

He would have stopped it. Wouldn't he?

Pause.

Wouldn't he?

AMANDA. He wasn't bloody Superman.

Silence.

BECKY. This is all your fault.

AMANDA. What?

BECKY. It's your fault.

Pause.

If you'd told Henderson straight away, made a fuss like you should have.

AMANDA. That's enough.

BECKY. Told him what Jason was like, stopped making excuses for him.

AMANDA. I never made excuses for him.

BECKY. Excuse me. Rewind. (*Mimicking*.) 'If you knew what I knew, African-Caribbean boys, blah, blah...'

AMANDA. Okay.

BECKY. You should have done something about it and you know it.

AMANDA. I told him. I told him what happened.

BECKY. Yeah. 'I don't want to get him in trouble... He was angry... I stood in front of him. Don't punish him. Give him a fucking sweetie.'

Pause.

You are seriously fucked up.

AMANDA. Thank you.

BECKY. I swear to God if Jason Chambers came and raped me now in front of you, you'd still think it wasn't his fault.

AMANDA. That's a disgusting thing to say.

BECKY. You'd probably say that I asked for it because my skirt's above the ankle.

AMANDA. Stop it.

BECKY. That really I should feel sorry for him and let him fuck me again.

AMANDA. Be quiet.

BECKY. Because that's what he's done to you, Mum. Hasn't he?

AMANDA. I'm warning you, Becky.

BECKY. He's well and truly fucked you over, hasn't he?

AMANDA. Shut up.

BECKY. But as Jason says –

AMANDA. Rebecca.

BECKY. You love a bit of black dick, don't you, Mum?

AMANDA turns away. BECKY looks on. Silence.

Mum.

AMANDA doesn't respond.

Mum.

Pause.

Mum.

She touches AMANDA's arm.

AMANDA. Don't touch me.

PETER walks in.

PETER. I got you this.

Puts a Kit Kat on the table in front of BECKY.

They didn't have the one with caramel in it. I think they were a limited edition or something.

Pause. He looks at them. Silence. PETER hands AMANDA the tablets and some water.

They only had caplets.

They all sit. Silence.

Does anyone want a drink?

Pause.

Cup of tea?

BECKY. No.

AMANDA (*to* BECKY). 'Thank you.'

Pause.

(*To* BECKY.) It's 'No, thank you.'

BECKY. No, thank you.

Silence.

AMANDA. I'm going to lie down.

PETER. Are you okay?

AMANDA. Yeah.

BECKY. Mum?

Pause.

Sorry.

She looks at her. She goes.

PETER *looks at* BECKY.

I didn't do anything.

PETER. I didn't say you did.

BECKY. I didn't say you said I did.

Pause.

(*She gets up.*) I've got homework.

Pause.

PETER. What are you sorry for?

BECKY. None of your fucking business.

She goes. PETER, *alone, eats the Kit Kat.*

Scene Eighteen

Under the stairs. JASON *and* DEE. *Sitting close.*

JASON. The others are going tonight. After school, innit.

She doesn't say anything. He strokes her hair. She shrugs him off.

What's the matter?

Pause.

What is it?

Pause.

Dee?

DEE. Nothin'.

Silence.

JASON. Just go with them.

Silence.

What?

Pause.

It's okay.

Silence.

What?

Pause.

DEE. It isn't.

JASON. If everyone says the same thing.

Silence.

DEE. Tell Henderson.

JASON. What?

DEE. Tell him.

Pause.

Please.

Pause.

I'll come with you.

Pause.

We can do it together.

Pause.

I'll help you, innit.

Pause.

Jas?

Pause.

Tell the truth, yeah?

Pause.

Everything will be alright.

Pause.

I promise.

Pause.

Whatever happens, it'll be alright.

Pause.

JASON. Just go in and say you want to give a statement. Tell them you was a witness. And then say what happened, yeah?

Pause. DEE *looks at him.* JASON *looks away.*

And when you go, make sure Chuggs ain't too much of a cunt.

FIRAT *enters. He stops and looks at them.*

FIRAT. It is very appalling what you have done.

Pause.

It is a terrible mistake.

DEE. What have we done?

Pause.

I said, what have we done?

FIRAT. Your lies have consequented a lot of upset.

JASON. Fuckin' speak English, man.

DEE. Nobody lied.

FIRAT. Rebecca is a nice person. She is not deserving of this.

JASON. She's a mouthy sket like her mother.

FIRAT. No.

JASON. No?

FIRAT. No.

JASON. She ain't ever going to fuck you. That ain't ever going to happen.

Pause.

FIRAT. It is too much. With the police. It is too much.

JASON. Shit, news travels fast, yeah?

FIRAT. I am going to speak to Mr Henderson.

JASON. What?

FIRAT. I am going to inform him what I saw.

JASON. But you never saw nothin'.

FIRAT. I am going to inform him what I heard.

JASON. But you never heard nothin', innit.

FIRAT. Yes.

JASON. You already told him.

FIRAT. I am going to tell him I saw everything. I heard everything. What you are saying is not the truth.

JASON. You was on the floor, shittin' yourself, cryin' about your glasses.

FIRAT. It would be better if you went to tell him first.

JASON. It's jokes, yeah?

FIRAT. If you tell him the truth, you will get in the less trouble.

JASON. I'm not telling him nothin', innit. You can't just go in and say you saw what happened when you never.

FIRAT. I know what happened.

JASON. You never fuckin' saw. You never fuckin' heard.

FIRAT. I know what happened.

JASON. Listen, yeah? He ain't going to believe you.

FIRAT. He said to come back if I remembered.

Pause.

I remembered.

JASON. You wanker.

FIRAT. I am sorry.

JASON. You will be.

FIRAT. I have to. For Rebecca.

JASON. I'm tellin' you, if you go up those stairs to that office, you will regret it. You get me?

Pause.

You live on Barclay Road, don't you? I seen you with your little sister. She's in Year Seven, ain't she? You walk to school together, innit.

Pause.

I will fuck you up. Do you understand what I am saying?

DEE. Rebecca ain't worth that, is she? Not when you don't know what really happened. Not when you can't be sure what the truth is.

JASON. Now turn around and fuckin' walk away.

FIRAT *turns around and walks away.*

Scene Nineteen

It is night. BECKY *goes quickly into the kitchen. She doesn't turn the light on. She opens the kitchen drawer and takes each knife out of the drawer, and places them onto the kitchen table in order of size – almost trance-like. She stands back and surveys her handiwork. She looks at them for a long time. Chooses one.* AMANDA *enters the scene in her dressing gown.*

She looks at BECKY. BECKY *looks back at her. She is frozen to the spot. They look at one another. An age.* AMANDA *moves to* BECKY *who is completely still. She looks at the table and at each knife and one by one she replaces them in the drawer.* BECKY *looks at the floor. When all the knives are in the drawer,* AMANDA *stands opposite* BECKY. *Tenderly, she moves a piece of* BECKY*'s hair from her face. She strokes her hair and kisses her face.* BECKY *is limp. She takes the knife from her hand and places it back in the drawer. She kisses* BECKY*'s wrists and arms and pulls her towards her and holds her tightly.*

BECKY *begins to cry.*

Scene Twenty

JASON*'s house. He is in night clothes – shorts and T-shirt. He is texting. Agitated. Puts phone down. He picks it up. Looks at it. Puts it down. He picks it up again. Texts. Puts it down. Silence. He picks it up, fiddles around with it. Gets up. Sits down. Puts it down. Picks it up. He dials.*

JASON. It's me again. Call me. As soon as you can, yeah?

He puts the phone on the table and he sits. A long time. He picks up the phone.

I just wanna know how it went. Don't matter how late it is, call me, yeah? I'm waitin'.

He sits. He texts. Puts his phone down. Picks it up and dials again.

Where are you? Where the fuck are you? I'm waitin' here like a fuckin' pussy. Fuckin' call me.

He puts the phone down and sits. He hears the front door. He quickly puts his phone away, tucking it into his shorts, and gets up to get a drink. BEN *walks in.*

BEN. Why aren't you in bed?

JASON. I was thirsty.

BEN (*taking the drink*). What have I said about that?

JASON goes to leave.

How was school?

JASON. Alright.

BEN. Did you hand that note in?

JASON. Yeah. Yes.

BEN. And what did they say?

JASON. Nothing.

BEN. What did your form tutor say?

JASON. Nothing.

BEN. Your form tutor didn't ask you why you'd been with the police?

JASON. No.

BEN. She didn't ask what you were doing there?

JASON. No.

BEN. She didn't mention it?

JASON. She probably already knows.

BEN. Did you hand it in?

JASON. Yes.

BEN. I told you to make sure you handed it in.

JASON. I did.

BEN *sits down. Silence.*

BEN. How was work, Dad? Fine, nice of you to ask.

Pause.

JASON. How was work?

BEN *tuts and shakes his head.*

What happened?

BEN. Nothing. Nothing ever happens.

Silence.

Some fool nearly drove into me on the way home.

Pause. JASON *goes to go.*

Where are you going? I'm talking to you. You don't just walk off when I'm in the middle of talking to you.

JASON. I thought you'd finished.

BEN. Does that sound like the end of the anecdote?

Pause.

Does it?

JASON. I don't know.

BEN. Do you even know what 'anecdote' means?

JASON. No.

BEN. It's not a difficult word.

JASON. I never heard it before.

BEN. What do you think it means?

JASON. I don't know.

BEN. Can't you work it out?

JASON *shrugs. Pause.*

It's when you retell something that happened to you, to make it interesting, like making it into a story.

Pause.

Know what I mean?

JASON. Yes.

BEN. So if I say some fool nearly drove into me, is that interesting?

JASON. Yes.

BEN. No, it's not. How can that be the end of the story? Do you really think that's the end of the story?

JASON. No.

BEN. So why were you going?

JASON. I'm tired, I've got school tomorrow and –

BEN. I was coming up Shernhall Road and he pulled out without even looking. He didn't even look. Just thought he had the road to himself. I drove up his arse all the way back, all the way. I was practically on top of him. I could see him in his mirror, scared, looking back all the time, wondering what I was going to do to him.

Silence. BEN *looks at* JASON *for a response.*

JASON. And then what happened?

Silence.

He shouldn't of pulled out in front of you.

BEN. No, he shouldn't.

JASON. He should of looked.

BEN. Treating me like a mug.

JASON*'s phone rings. They look at each other.* JASON *looks at it. He rejects it.*

What have I told you about that?

JASON. Sorry.

BEN. What's the rule?

Pause.

JASON. No calls after ten.

BEN. It's twenty past twelve.

JASON. Sorry.

BEN. How can you learn anything at school if you're up all night on the phone?

JASON. I'm not.

BEN. Don't lie to me.

JASON. I'm not, I –

BEN. Has someone just called you?

JASON. Yeah. Yes.

BEN. What time is it?

JASON. Twenty past twelve.

BEN. And would you have answered it if I wasn't here?

Pause.

Think about it.

Pause.

JASON. Yes.

BEN. Yes what?

JASON. Yes, I'd answer it.

BEN. You think you can do what you want.

JASON. I don't.

BEN. You think I'm just some fool who pays the bills and buys your food.

JASON. No, I –

BEN. Some dickhead who works all hours so you can do what you want, never listening to a word I say.

JASON. I do.

BEN. If you had listened to me, we wouldn't find ourselves in the middle of this.

JASON. I never did nothing.

BEN. You represent me when you step out that door. Me, do you understand? And when you mess up, like you constantly mess up the simplest thing, like not handing a note in when I tell you, it makes me look a cunt.

Pause.

JASON. Sorry.

BEN *looks at him. Silence.*

Sorry.

Silence.

Dad, I'm sorry.

BEN. Stop saying that.

JASON. But I am, I'm –

BEN. Shut your mouth.

The phone rings again. BEN *takes the phone.*

You might act the big man out there in front of your little girlfriend, but you're just a little boy and you need to start listening, do you understand?

Pause.

I said –

JASON. Yes.

BEN. Yes what?

JASON. Yes, I understand.

Pause.

BEN. Do you think your rudeboys would think you were such a man if they knew what a pathetic kid you really are? Well?

Pause.

If they knew the truth about what a baby they were dealing with? Do you?

Pause.

It's a question. A question requires an answer. Now answer me.

Pause.

Fucking answer me, you pussy, you dirty little –

The phone rings again. JASON *goes to get it.* BEN *answers it.*

Hello, no, he can't speak to you. No, he's not available… It's too late… What's your name?… Can I ask you something?… Did you know that Jason pisses his bed?… I said, did you know that Jason pisses himself at night?… You shouldn't be calling. It's too late. Don't call again.

He puts the phone down.

I am it for you. I'm all you've got so you better fix up and start making some better fucking choices.

Scene Twenty-One

CHRIS *is sitting*. AMANDA *stands*.

CHRIS. I'm sorry.

AMANDA. Is that it?

CHRIS. It's –

AMANDA. Don't tell me it's procedure.

CHRIS. But –

AMANDA. If you tell me it's procedure, I might just bite your face off.

Pause.

Is it because the police are involved? Is that why?

CHRIS. Amanda, I can't talk about it.

AMANDA. Is it because of the meeting, the strategy meeting?

CHRIS. Speak to your union representative.

AMANDA. What did the social worker say? Did she mention Brighton? Did they say something about Becky's dad?

CHRIS. I can't talk about it.

AMANDA. They did, didn't they? It's about that meeting at Becky's primary in Brighton, isn't it, when she stopped talking? That's why, isn't it?

Silence.

CHRIS. You shouldn't be here. By rights, reception shouldn't even have let you in.

AMANDA. By rights, I should be teaching Year Seven now.

CHRIS. Until the police have finished, there's nothing I can do.

AMANDA. Brilliant.

CHRIS. We can't jeopardise a criminal investigation.

AMANDA. Life goes on, eh? Business as usual while I'm stuck at home waiting for a social worker to come knocking. Better hide all the booze bottles, eh?

CHRIS. Amanda, I can't speak about this any more. You can't come here and you can't ask me about it.

AMANDA. Thanks.

CHRIS. I know it's difficult –

AMANDA. Do you?

CHRIS. Yes, I do, and I think it's important to be as transparent as possible at this point.

Pause.

When all the agencies, the police, social services, have done what they need to do, there may be – and I mean may, it's not definite – but there could be some kind of disciplinary hearing in school.

AMANDA. But if the police drop the –

CHRIS. It's pro–

AMANDA. Don't say it.

CHRIS. I have to be impartial, so when it's time, George will lead the school's investigation –

AMANDA. George?

CHRIS. Yes. It's important that I'm not involved, so I've spoken to George and he'll be in touch when –

AMANDA. George Cooper?

CHRIS. Yes.

AMANDA. George Cooper who can't be arsed to leave his office unless there's a doughnut in the staffroom.

CHRIS. George is very experienced.

AMANDA. Experienced at doing sod all.

CHRIS. If I didn't think he was up to it –

AMANDA. I'd feel more reassured if the bloody caretaker was investigating.

CHRIS. He's been a deputy for twenty years.

AMANDA. Yeah, fat wages for sitting on his fat arse for twenty years. When Mike went, George didn't exactly trip over himself to take on the acting headship, did he? Because that might have meant he'd have to do some bloody work.

CHRIS. Alright, Amanda.

AMANDA. So you do nothing to help me and then you hand it over to George, who'll carry on doing nothing.

CHRIS. That's not fair.

AMANDA. Isn't it?

CHRIS. George is already thinking about the best way to proceed. He's suggested meeting all the parents of the kids involved.

Pause.

AMANDA. You should have done that, right at the start. I said that to you.

CHRIS. I don't remember you saying that.

AMANDA. That's what you should have done, isn't it? Got the parents in. Interviewed the kids with their parents.

CHRIS. You have to go.

AMANDA. Why didn't you?

CHRIS. Amanda, I'm not to blame.

AMANDA. Why didn't you do that? Why didn't you get their parents in?

CHRIS. I'm trying to do the best for everyone involved.

AMANDA. I've got a social worker coming to see me next week to assess whether I'm a risk to my own daughter.

CHRIS. I know.

AMANDA. How is that 'best for everyone involved'?

CHRIS. That's not down to me.

AMANDA. If you'd got the parents sooner –

CHRIS. I can't discuss this. You have to leave.

AMANDA. No.

Pause.

I'm not going.

CHRIS. I know this is all very upsetting.

AMANDA. I'm not going.

CHRIS. Amanda.

AMANDA. Knowing that you've just washed your hands of the whole thing.

CHRIS. I haven't.

AMANDA. Delegating to George because it's all got a bit bloody messy. You can forget it if you think I'm going to crawl away in a whisper and let a group of stupid vindictive teenagers and that lazy work-shy bastard George –

CHRIS. Calm down.

AMANDA. I trusted you to sort this out.

CHRIS. I tried. I'm trying.

AMANDA. I trusted you.

CHRIS. I'm doing the best I can.

AMANDA. And look where that's got us.

CHRIS. Listen, I never wanted this bloody job. I'm doing it because no one else will.

AMANDA. *Is that supposed to make me feel sorry for you? I couldn't give a shit about how you feel about your job.*

CHRIS. Go home, Amanda.

AMANDA. I'm going to go downstairs and I'm going to get those kids and I'm going to bring them up here and I'm going to make them tell the truth.

CHRIS. You can't do that.

AMANDA. What choice do I have?

CHRIS. You have to go.

AMANDA. Tell me, Chris, because I've run right out of ideas. Tell me, what I should do. What should I do?

CHRIS. Now. You have to go now.

AMANDA. I will not allow this to happen to me. I will not allow you to let it happen. I will not allow it.

CHRIS. If you don't leave now, I'm going to call the police.

Scene Twenty-Two

BECKY *is sitting at the kitchen table in her school uniform. She has a glass of milk and is spooning Nesquik Chocolate powder into it. She digs her spoon in and then levels off the powder and adds it to the milk. She gets up and goes to the kitchen drawer, opens it, looks inside and leaves it open. She returns to the Nesquik and continues adding it to the milk. She glances at the drawer. Puts the spoon down. Puts her head on the table. A long time.* PETER *comes in, ready for work. He looks at* BECKY *to see if she's asleep. Goes up really close to her, trying not to wake her. She suddenly looks up right into his face.*

BECKY (*starts*). Fuck! What are you doing?

PETER (*jumping back*). Jesus Christ, you nearly gave me a heart attack.

BECKY. You nearly gave me a fucking heart attack.

PETER. I was trying to see if you were asleep.

He puts the kettle on, gets cereal, etc.

Want one?

She taps her glass with the spoon.

BECKY. No thanks.

PETER. That doesn't look very nutritious. Shall I do you some toast?

BECKY. No thanks.

He makes his tea and sits down. They sit in silence.

PETER. You're a bit late.

She nods.

BECKY. Where's Mum?

PETER. She's gone to see Chris. You finding it hard to sleep?

She nods.

You've never been a good sleeper, have you?

BECKY. Sleep's overrated anyway.

She measures some Nesquik and stirs it into the milk. She takes spoonfuls and starts making little piles on the kitchen table. He watches.

Do you remember when you first met me?

PETER. Yes.

BECKY. What was I like?

PETER. Sad.

BECKY. What did I say to you?

PETER. Nothing.

BECKY. Nothing?

PETER. Don't you remember?

She shakes her head.

You didn't speak. For six months.

BECKY. For six months?

PETER. You had everyone very worried. Don't you remember?

They sit in silence. She continues to make piles of Nesquik. He puts a cornflake on each pile. She looks at his hands.

BECKY. Did you ever see the old pier in Brighton?

PETER. Yeah.

BECKY. My dad was obsessed by it.

PETER. Was he?

BECKY. He was always going on about how it was deteriorating. He used to take a photo of it every week so he had a record of it falling down. What a weirdo.

PETER. I guess we all have our –

BECKY. I've got this photo of me and him standing in front of it. This really old woman took it. Dad asked her to and she was shaking because she was nervous in case she took it wrong. He bought her a cup of tea after and he kept making her laugh calling her 'lady in red' and 'scarlet woman' because she had this red coat on. He could be really cheesy sometimes. I mean really fucking cheesy.

Pause.

And then we walked her back to her house and when we got there, she bent right down and took my hand and said, 'You're very lucky to have such a wonderful daddy.'

Pause.

Talk about cheesy. That is cheese on toast. That whole story is mature cheddar on a piece of poor-little-me toast.

PETER. It's not. It's lovely.

Pause.

BECKY. If I close my eyes, I can see that woman so clearly. I can remember everything about her. Everything.

Pause.

But when I think of Dad, I can't see him. It's like he's getting further and further away from me and the more I try, the more I try to imagine, the more I look at photos of him to try and remember, the stranger he looks.

Pause.

PETER. Your mum said he loved you very much.

BECKY. I don't think so.

PETER. He did.

Pause.

BECKY. Did Mum tell you about the tie?

Pause.

PETER. You're an amazing girl, Becky. A brave funny clever girl.

BECKY. And you're a soppy loser.

PETER. At least we agree on that.

BECKY. When we got the pictures back, she'd cut his head off. In the photo I'm holding hands with a headless man.

Pause.

PETER. Do you want a lift to school?

BECKY. It's alright, I'll get the bus with the rest of the plebs.

AMANDA *enters*.

AMANDA (*to* BECKY). What are you still doing here?

PETER. Amanda.

AMANDA. Get to school.

BECKY. I'm going.

AMANDA. Hurry up then.

BECKY. Alright.

AMANDA. What's all this mess?

BECKY. It's art, what does it fucking look like?

She goes into her room.

AMANDA. For God's sake, Peter, we need to try and keep everything as normal as possible.

PETER. She's worried.

AMANDA. We're all worried.

PETER. She can't sleep.

AMANDA. It doesn't do her any good letting her stay off school.

PETER. She's going.

AMANDA. She didn't look like she was in any particular hurry.

PETER. She was going.

AMANDA. You need to parent her.

PETER. Give me a break.

AMANDA. She doesn't need a friend.

PETER. She does.

AMANDA. Spare me. That's the bloody easy part.

   Pause.

PETER. I take it seeing Chris didn't go so well.

AMANDA. That's an understatement.

PETER. I did try to warn you.

AMANDA. Very helpful. Thank you.

   Pause. He goes to her.

PETER. We just need to wait.

AMANDA. Yes.

PETER. We have to be patient.

AMANDA. Yes.

PETER. When are you going to tell Becky?

AMANDA. I don't know.

PETER. Sooner rather than later, don't you think?

AMANDA. I don't know.

BECKY (*coming back in*). Tell me what?

   Pause.

   What?

   Pause. PETER *and* AMANDA *look at each other.*

   What?

AMANDA. I've had a phone call from social services. They want to visit us.

BECKY. What for?

AMANDA. To make sure everything is alright.

BECKY. What do you mean?

Pause.

PETER. They just want to make sure you're okay.

BECKY. What?

PETER. Safe. Here. With us.

AMANDA. With me.

BECKY. Why?

PETER. Because of the allegation.

BECKY (*to* AMANDA). Do they think you're hurting me?

PETER. They just have to be sure. That's all. They'll talk to all of us.

BECKY. And what if they decide I'm not safe?

AMANDA. Don't be silly, love.

BECKY. What if they take me away?

PETER. They won't.

AMANDA. It's not going to happen.

BECKY. You said those cunts wouldn't lie and they did.

AMANDA. Don't say that word.

BECKY. What, 'lie'?

PETER. They just want to talk to us.

BECKY. Who's going to look after me?

AMANDA. Stop it.

BECKY (*to* PETER). Will you? If they won't let me live with Mum?

PETER. It's not going to come to that.

BECKY. Will you, though? Will you?

PETER. It's not going to happen.

BECKY. You don't want to. He doesn't want to.

AMANDA. Becky.

PETER. Of course I'd look after you.

BECKY. But you don't really want to.

PETER. I do.

BECKY. Not fucking really, though.

AMANDA. That's enough.

BECKY. Even though you think I'm amazing.

AMANDA. Please.

BECKY. And what else was there? Brave, funny. What was the other one? Clever, yeah, a fucking genius, that's me. You think I'm the icing on the cake, the Queen of England, the dog's bollocks, but you don't really mean it, do you? You don't mean any of it. You couldn't really give a shit.

PETER. Have you finished?

BECKY. No, I don't think I have. Because you're a –

AMANDA. Shut up. Just shut your mouth. You never know when to fucking stop. This is not all about you, you selfish cow. Shut your fucking mouth or I swear to fucking God, I'll...

Silence.

Sorry.

Pause.

I'm sorry.

Pause.

Becky, I'm so sorry.

Silence.

I hate him. I hate his guts. Every single part of me hates him. I felt sorry for him. I've always felt sorry for him because of his mum, but it's no excuse. I hate him. I hate all of them.

PETER. It's understandable, love, you –

AMANDA. I don't feel like myself any more. I don't feel like me. I don't feel like I know who I am.

Pause.

BECKY. What about her?

Pause.

AMANDA. What?

BECKY. Jason's mum.

Pause.

AMANDA. Nothing.

Pause.

I shouldn't have said anything.

BECKY. No, of course not.

AMANDA. I shouldn't.

BECKY. Why are you still protecting him?

AMANDA. I'm not.

BECKY. After everything he's done.

AMANDA. I can't tell you.

BECKY. What's the big secret?

AMANDA. It's not a big secret. It's just –

BECKY (*to* PETER). Do you know?

PETER *looks at* AMANDA.

Why is everyone allowed to know what's going on except me?

AMANDA. Everyone doesn't know.

BECKY. Oh sorry, I forgot, I can't be trusted.

AMANDA. It's not that.

BECKY. Course not.

AMANDA. Becky.

BECKY. Forget it, I don't care anyway, why should I?

Pause.

AMANDA. She killed herself.

Pause. BECKY *stops for a moment.*

When he was in Year Four.

Pause.

BECKY. So what?

Scene Twenty-Three

Under the stairs. CHUGGS, SAIF, CHLOE, DEE *and* JASON *all standing up.*

JASON. I called you.

Pause.

All of you. Where was you?

Pause.

DEE. I rang you. I spoke to your dad…

He puts a finger up to silence her.

JASON. I was waitin', innit.

CHLOE. I never had my phone. Mr Richardson took it off of me yesterday in art. He's such a prick, man. With his stupid moustache and his paintbrushes.

CHUGGS. They was fuckin' rude. Talked to us like we was spastic retards.

SAIF. They said they didn't need our help.

CHLOE. They said they couldn't talk about it.

DEE. We tried, innit.

SAIF. Innit.

CHUGGS. We did, bruv. We did.

CHLOE. Dee was funny, man, she was all flirting up to the feds and that.

Pause.

Only cos she wanted to give her statement. Not cos –

CHUGGS. He was a old man. That one writing out that paper.

SAIF. They said it would be better if we stayed out of it, innit.

JASON. Is it?

SAIF. Yeah. Innit, Dee?

DEE. Yeah.

CHUGGS. That old one was eating a Big Mac. It gave me the munch so we went McDonald's after, innit.

SAIF. Then went over the park.

JASON. Why didn't you answer my calls?

Pause.

SAIF. We knew you'd be bare pissed off, innit.

CHUGGS. I was playing football with this Albanian kid. He was well good. He was only about fucking ten or something. He was sick.

Pause.

DEE. We thought… I thought it would be better if I told you.

Pause.

JASON. And is it better?

Pause.

Is it?

Pause.

CHLOE. Look, man, we did our best, innit. We did what you said. We tried. It weren't our fault.

Silence.

JASON. What did Jordon do?

SAIF. What do you mean?

JASON. After you went to the police.

CHUGGS. He came park with us, innit.

JASON. What about his sister?

CHLOE. What about her?

JASON. Did she go to the park with youse?

CHLOE. Why would she come to the park?

JASON. So he took her home?

CHLOE. She was never with us.

    Pause.

JASON. But Jordon was there, innit?

CHLOE. Yeah, Jordon was there.

    Pause.

JASON. You never went, did you?

DEE. What?

SAIF. What?

CHUGGS. We did, fam.

JASON. Nah. Nah. You never.

CHLOE. Why would we lie for?

JASON. That's why you never answered my calls.

DEE. I called you. Your dad –

JASON. Shut the fuck up.

SAIF. Jas, we went. We did.

JASON. Nah, nah, this is bullshit.

CHLOE. What's he chattin' about?

JASON (*to* SAIF). You told them not to go, innit.

SAIF. No.

JASON. I don't believe you.

CHUGGS. He never told us nothin'.

SAIF. Whatever, man.

JASON. Because you's a pussy and you fuckin' shook, got 'em all shook.

CHUGGS. No, man, you got it wrong.

JASON. Fuck you, idiot.

CHLOE. Don't talk to him like –

JASON. You can fuck off as well.

CHLOE. What?

JASON. Thinking you's ripe. You's just a stupid little girl who can't keep her mouth shut.

SAIF. Jas, come on, man.

JASON. Or her legs.

DEE. Allow it.

CHLOE. Fuck you.

JASON (*to* DEE). What, you think she your friend? She's always up on me as soon as you walkin' away. (*Gets his phone.*) Have a look, see what a nice friend you got? (*He looks at the phone.*) Here's one.

CHLOE *goes to grab the phone. He pushes her away.*

(*Reading.*) 'You look fit today.'

CHLOE (*trying to get it*). You bastard.

JASON. What? It ain't true, Chloe? (*In her face.*) You's a dirty sket.

SAIF (*pulling him away*). Leave her, man, she ain't done nothin'.

JASON. Like all of youse.

Pause.

Got my back? Yeah fuckin' right. Yeah. Jokes, innit.

SAIF. We did what you said.

JASON. I thought out of all of them, you –

SAIF. Like we always do what you say. We tried, innit.

JASON. Yeah, yeah, I heard. And I heard the Disney tale that you went to McDonald's and the park and Chuggs played football with an Albanian kid. I heard you. And you know what, it's all shit.

SAIF. Fuck this.

JASON. Got all your stories straight.

DEE. Jas, that's not how it is.

JASON. Don't speak to me. You call five hours later to break the bad news, enough time for all the fuckin' stories to get sorted, innit, so don't fuckin' speak to me.

SAIF. You've lost it. I'm goin'. Laters, man.

He starts walking away.

JASON. That's right, walk on. Yeah. Remember, though, remember when you teafed that iPod and I took the blame, yeah? Remember when the South T boys was after you, yeah? And how I had your back? Remember –

SAIF (*turns back*). I can't keep owin' you, man.

CHUGGS. Innit.

SAIF. If this is what it's going to be like, yeah, I don't wanna be your bredrin. I feel like your bitch.

CHUGGS. It's truth, man.

JASON (*up to* SAIF). Is it?

SAIF. Yeah.

JASON (*in his face*). Is it?

SAIF. Yeah, it is.

DEE. Allow it, Jas.

JASON. Nah, nah. I got my bitch here. And she gonna bark.

CHUGGS. Don't, man.

JASON (*in his face*). Bark, bitch.

SAIF. I ain't scared of you.

DEE. Leave it, Saif. Just go, yeah.

SAIF. You think you can control us all, yeah?

JASON. Yeah?

SAIF. You's always been like this.

JASON. Is it?

SAIF. Even when we was small. Even before your mum.

JASON *grabs him by the throat.*

JASON. Don't fuckin' talk about my mum. You get me?

CHUGGS. What the fuck?

CHLOE. Get off him. Stop it, man, stop it.

JASON. Do you understand what I'm sayin'? Do you? Do you?

DEE. Leave him. Jason, don't.

JASON. Don't you ever talk about my mum.

DEE. Stop it. Get off him.

CHUGGS. Allow it, man.

JASON. You hear me? Yeah?

CHLOE. Leave him.

DEE. Get the fuck off him.

DEE *tries to pull his arm off* SAIF. JASON *turns round and grabs hold of her by her hair. They all stop.* DEE *sinks to the ground. Shock. Silence.*

CHLOE (*to* DEE). Are you alright?

DEE *nods. They look at* JASON.

JASON. I...

Pause.

SAIF. No, man.

CHUGGS. Nah. Nah.

CHUGGS helps DEE up.

JASON. Dee, man, I didn't...

CHLOE puts her arm around DEE.

CHLOE. Let's go, innit.

DEE shrugs her off.

SAIF (*to* JASON). What the fuck is wrong with you?

JASON. I didn't mean to.

SAIF. Yeah, whatever. Dee? You comin'?

DEE stares at JASON.

Dee?

DEE stares at JASON. SAIF, CHUGGS and CHLOE walk away, leaving JASON and DEE alone.

JASON. I'm sorry.

She looks at him.

It was an accident.

She looks at him.

Dee, I never meant to.

Pause.

Dee, listen, I'm sorry. I'm really fuckin' sorry.

Pause.

Dee, please.

Pause.

Please.

Pause.

DEE. Is it true what your dad said?

JASON. What?

DEE. Your dad, on the phone, last night, he said –

JASON. I know what he said.

Pause.

DEE. Is it true?

Pause.

JASON. Course it ain't true. What do you think I am? How can you ask me? How can you fuckin' ask me?

She looks at him and then walks away.

Dee. I'm sorry. Dee.

He is left alone. JORDON *enters.*

JORDON. Alright?

JASON *doesn't answer.*

Where is everyone?

JASON. Dunno.

JORDON. You seen Chloe today?

JASON. Yeah.

JORDON. She tell you about Dee all sexing up to the old police officer man?

Pause.

It was sick, man. Bare jokes.

Pause.

JASON. Did your sister get her sweets?

JORDON. Huh?

JASON. Your sister?

JORDON. Oh nah, my auntie took her in the end. I didn't think it was right, innit, her being with feds. She only six. Give her another ten years before they meet her, innit.

JORDON's *phone starts beeping. He reads it. He looks at* JASON.

I gotta go, man.

JASON. Is it?

JORDON. Yeah, bro. Laters, man. Keep the peace.

He runs off. JASON sits. He takes his phone out. Thinks about sending a text. Starts it. Puts it away and just sits. BECKY walks on. He looks up. She stares at him. He looks away. She sits down next to him. Silence.

BECKY. You should have said it was an accident.

Pause.

You should have said that you didn't realise she was a teacher. You thought she was a kid, that she got in your way.

Pause.

You should have said you were angry. God, everyone would believe that.

Silence.

When I was in Year Three, I had Mrs Vaughan, do you remember her?

JASON. No.

BECKY. You were in Year Four. Who was your teacher?

JASON. Dunno.

BECKY. Was it Mrs Stapleton?

He shrugs.

Why do you do that?

Pause.

Act like you don't know it was Mrs Stapleton.

JASON. What are you chattin' about?

BECKY. It's weird.

Pause.

She had that sock puppet. She'd make it talk to you and whisper in your ear. Do you remember? What was it called?

Pause.

You must remember.

JASON. I don't fuckin' know.

BECKY. Bobby. Yeah, that was it. Bobby. Bobby Sox. I loved Bobby Sox.

Pause.

If you were upset, she used to put on that accent and sing that song.

Pause.

Do you remember?

JASON. No.

Pause.

BECKY *sings the first verse of 'Bring Me Sunshine', the signature tune of Eric Morecambe and Ernie Wise.*

She looks at him.

Freak.

BECKY. Tell Henderson it was a mistake.

JASON. There ain't no such thing as a mistake.

BECKY. What?

JASON. That's what my dad says, innit.

BECKY. That's not true.

JASON. It's what he says.

BECKY. I'll come with you.

JASON. Why would I want you to do that?

BECKY. I dunno, support, whatever.

JASON. I don't need your support, innit. Save it for your mum.

BECKY. If you knew what you'd done.

JASON. I don't give a fuck.

BECKY. You've got everyone involved in this, making everyone do what you want.

JASON. Innit.

BECKY. Manipulating them.

JASON. Yeah.

BECKY. Lying for you.

JASON. Yeah.

BECKY. How can you admit it like that? Like it's nothing. Like it doesn't matter.

JASON. It don't.

BECKY. Course it matters.

JASON. It don't.

BECKY. A social worker is going to interview me.

Pause.

To see if my mum hits me.

JASON. Does she?

BECKY. Course she doesn't.

JASON. That's all right then, innit.

BECKY. She's not allowed in school. She might never be able to teach again and she loves teaching.

JASON. I don't give a shit about you or your mum.

Pause.

BECKY. She always liked you, you know.

Pause.

You could stop this right now.

JASON. Yeah.

BECKY. Stop it then.

Pause.

Why not?

JASON. I don't want to, innit.

BECKY. You can't treat people like this. You can't treat me –

JASON. I can do what I want.

BECKY. I know about your mum.

Pause.

I know how you feel.

He looks at her.

I know exactly how you feel.

JASON. You don't.

BECKY. I do.

Silence.

Do you ever wake up and think she's still alive?

JASON. No.

BECKY. And for a moment, just before you open your eyes, everything seems alright.

JASON. No.

BECKY. Do you have that dream where you're screaming, but no sound comes out?

JASON. No.

BECKY. It's hard not to think that if you'd done something differently, maybe –

JASON. No.

BECKY. My dad used the tie I gave him for Christmas.

He looks at her.

It had Homer Simpson on it. D'oh.

JASON. That ain't funny.

BECKY. Do you think it was your fault?

JASON. No.

BECKY. Sometimes I think it was mine.

JASON. It weren't.

BECKY. How do you know?

Pause.

Sometimes I can't breathe. I feel like something's pushing on my chest, trying to get out and I don't know what it is. Do you know what I mean?

JASON (*starts laughing*). No.

BECKY. Why are you laughing?

JASON. You chat such shit.

BECKY. You know what I'm talking about. I know you –

JASON (*laughing*). I ain't got no clue what you's on about, innit.

BECKY. I don't believe you.

JASON. You don't know nothin' about me. You's a silly little Goth girl. We ain't the same. We ain't ever gonna be the same. You ain't got a clue. I don't give a shit if your dad's dead. I don't give a shit if your mum loses her job.

BECKY. Shut up.

JASON. I don't give a fuck if they take you away and put you in care and you never see your mum again. It makes no fuckin' difference to me at all, innit.

BECKY. You're a bastard.

JASON. You mean a black bastard.

BECKY. It's not a joke. It's not a fucking joke.

JASON. You's a fuckin' joke. You think singin' a song from primary is gonna get me to Henderson? Chattin' shit about back in the day. Tellin' me about your dad as if I give a fuck.

She takes off her sweatbands and rolls up her sleeves. She shows him her arms.

They are a criss-cross of scars.

BECKY. This is what I do.

Pause.

When I can't stand it any more.

Pause.

JASON (*laughs*). I bet your bedroom's painted black as well, innit.

She unbuttons her trousers.

What the fuck you doing?

She pulls her down her trousers and lifts up her shirt. Her thighs are covered in raised scars, scabs and blood. Much, much worse.

BECKY. This is what I do.

He looks away.

Look.

Pause.

It's disgusting, isn't it?

She pulls up her trousers.

What do you do?

Pause.

When you can't bear it?

Pause.

Jason?

Silence.

How did your mum do it?

Pause.

When she couldn't stand it any more?

Pause.

Jason?

JASON. Be quiet.

BECKY. I told you how my dad did it. It's only fair.

Pause.

Did she do it with a rope?

Pause.

No?

Pause.

A scarf? A belt? Shoelaces?

Pause.

That's it. She did it with your shoelaces. Box-fresh.

Pause.

Maybe it was pills. Did she go to Superdrug? Get herself a bumper pack? Two for the price of one. Do it cheap as possible. No expense spared.

JASON. Shut up.

BECKY. She probably went for something quick. Get it over and done with.

JASON. Shut your mouth.

BECKY. Pills take a bit of time. Someone might have found her. Revived her. She wouldn't want that, would she?

JASON. You don't know what you're talkin' about.

BECKY. Wouldn't want to be stuck with you, would she?

JASON. Shut the fuck up.

BECKY. Don't fucking tell me what to do.

JASON. Fuck you.

BECKY. Did she slice her wrists?

JASON. You bitch.

BECKY. Slit her throat? To be sure.

JASON. You fuckin' bitch.

BECKY. To be sure that she never had to look at your nasty fucking face ever again.

JASON *goes right up to her. They are face to face. Eye to eye.*

What's the matter, Jason? Didn't your mummy love you?

He lunges at her, his fist raised. He holds her by the neck,
breathing, looking deep into her eyes.

Do it. It's what you do best, isn't it?

They look at each other. FIRAT *enters. He stops.*

FIRAT. Your girlfriend is with Mr Henderson.

JASON *slowly lets go of her. He backs away.*

She is in his office.

JASON *turns and walks away.* FIRAT *moves to* BECKY. *He*
lifts up her wrists and looks at them.

She lets him. He picks up her sweatbands and puts them on
her. He rolls down her sleeves and buttons them for her.
BECKY *remains in the same position under the stairs with*
FIRAT.

BECKY*'s phone rings. She answers.*

BECKY. Hi, Mum…

Scene Twenty-Four

CHRIS*'s office.* BEN *and* CHRIS.

CHRIS. It's permanent.

Pause.

Of course, you can appeal on Jason's behalf. But I'm sure
you know that.

Pause.

It's very unlikely it will be overturned.

BEN. I've contacted my solicitor.

CHRIS. That's your prerogative.

Pause.

If it was me, I wouldn't –

BEN. It isn't.

Pause.

CHRIS. I sometimes wonder how many parents would bother contesting exclusions if they had to pay the lawyers themselves. Legal aid, it's a beautiful thing, eh?

BEN. He's entitled.

CHRIS. 'Entitled.' Now there's a word I hear a lot.

Pause.

Jason's history, his past behaviour, obviously counted against him.

BEN. Obviously.

CHRIS. We have over a hundred documented incidents.

BEN. Is that right?

CHRIS. Since Year Seven.

Pause.

BEN. We have fifteen days to appeal, am I right?

CHRIS. Yes.

Pause.

I wonder what appealing the exclusion says to Jason. What does it show him?

Pause.

Children need to take responsibility for their actions.

Pause.

Mr Chambers?

BEN. Don't tell me how to parent.

Silence.

Do you know what percentage of black boys who are excluded end up in prison?

CHRIS. That can't influence the school's decision.

BEN. Do you?

CHRIS. He assaulted a member of staff and he lied.

BEN. Allegedly.

CHRIS. He's caused a lot of upset that could easily have been avoided.

BEN. And what about his exams?

CHRIS. We'll make arrangements for him to sit his exams elsewhere. The borough has a very good PRU.

BEN. He's not going to a pupil referral unit.

CHRIS. He can't come back.

BEN. You mean you won't let him.

Pause.

CHRIS. All the students have withdrawn their statements.

Pause.

All of them.

BEN. I can imagine how that happened.

CHRIS. Can you?

BEN. Yes.

Silence.

CHRIS. The police are dropping the investigation, have you been informed?

Silence.

Miss Phillips deserves an apology.

BEN. No.

CHRIS. This has been very difficult for her. Jason has –

BEN. No.

CHRIS. It's worth thinking about.

BEN. He's not apologising.

CHRIS. For Jason's sake. You know, to give him some, for want of a better word, without getting all American about it, closure, to give him some closure.

BEN. Permanent exclusion is closure. Closing down his future is closure.

CHRIS. It doesn't have to be like that.

Silence.

Why do you suppose he lied?

Pause.

Children do, that's not unusual. But it is unusual for them to see it through. They usually tell the truth in the end, usually in front of their parents.

Pause.

It's the point at which they can't hold on to the lie any longer.

Silence.

I think we've finished here. Unless there's anything else?

Pause.

Mr Chambers?

BEN. No.

CHRIS. I'll wait to hear from your solicitor.

BEN. Yes.

Pause.

CHRIS. Mr Chambers.

BEN. What?

CHRIS. People make mistakes.

Pause.

Children make mistakes. Teenagers make a lot of mistakes, believe me.

BEN. And?

CHRIS. It's important they understand that there are consequences. This could be the wake-up call that Jason needs. He's a bright boy and –

BEN. You think so, do you?

CHRIS. Yes. I do.

Pause.

Don't be too hard on him.

Scene Twenty-Five

JASON*'s house. He is sitting at the table. His school uniform is neatly folded up on the kitchen table.*

His phone is on the table. It rings. He looks at the caller. He lets it ring. It rings off. A moment later the same – he lets it ring. The third time, he picks up.

JASON. I didn't hear it... No, I was in the other room... No, I couldn't hear it, I was watching TV... I don't know, some-thing about... Nothing. I wasn't really watching. It was just on... I didn't hear... Sorry. Okay... Yeah... Sorry, I mean yes. What did he say?... I'm sorry... Yes... I know... Are you coming back now?... Yes... okay... Yes.

He puts the phone down. He sits for a long time. He looks around the room. He looks at the time. He picks up his school tie. He sits. He looks at the time. He looks at the tie. He looks at the ceiling. He winds the tie around his hands. He looks up. His phone rings. He lets it.

Scene Twenty-Six

CHRIS *'s office*. CHRIS *and* AMANDA.

AMANDA. What's going to happen to them?

CHRIS. They've admitted it.

AMANDA. You said.

CHRIS. All of them.

AMANDA. You said.

CHRIS. Except Jason. He's still… well, we've got rid of him. He's irrelevant. He'll appeal, but he hasn't got a ratshit chance in Hell. You don't need to worry about him.

AMANDA. I'm not.

CHRIS. You're free to come back.

AMANDA. Yes.

CHRIS. Tomorrow if you like. I know your Year Elevens have missed you. Monique Stewart keeps asking me when you're coming back. Every time I look up, there she is with her big starey eyes clutching her coursework and whispering your name. She's like a bloody stalker. I'd be careful if I were you.

Pause.

That was a joke.

Silence.

Or if you want a few more days to get yourself together we can arrange cover if that's what you'd prefer.

Silence.

I always believed you.

AMANDA. Okay.

CHRIS. I want you to know that.

AMANDA. Okay.

CHRIS. Everyone knows what happened.

AMANDA. Yes.

CHRIS. Everyone always knew that it was bollocks.

AMANDA. Did they?

CHRIS. You know they did. Everyone knows what Jason's like. And the others.

AMANDA. What's going to happen?

CHRIS. What?

AMANDA. To the others.

CHRIS. They've told the truth.

AMANDA. Yes.

CHRIS. And Jason's gone.

AMANDA. It wasn't just him.

CHRIS. He made them lie.

AMANDA. They knew what they were doing.

CHRIS. They've all had a detention with me.

Pause.

And their parents have been informed. Saif Anwar's went bloody ballistic. I thought I was going to have to do another child protection referral then and there.

Pause.

That was another joke.

AMANDA. It's nothing really, is it?

CHRIS. What?

AMANDA. A head-teacher's detention. An hour of staring into space on a Friday afternoon.

CHRIS. I can't exclude them all.

Pause.

Excluding six kids in one go will raise eyebrows. Excluding four other black kids, even temporarily, will give Miriam Harris's flunkies a fucking heart attack. Ofsted will be on the stats in a blink.

AMANDA. Saif's Asian.

CHRIS. I can't just exclude him. What would that look like?

Pause.

And we have permanently excluded Jason.

AMANDA. So you keep saying.

Pause.

CHRIS. It's enough, don't you think? We need to draw a line under this. Sometimes in this job we –

DEE *stands in the doorway.* CHRIS *looks at her. Pause.* AMANDA *turns round.*

DEE. I saw you come in. I was in maths. I saw you through the window.

Pause.

I saw you drive in in your car.

Pause.

I got permission from Mr Harvey. He said it was okay. He gave me his pass.

Pause.

I wanted to see you.

Pause.

To say sorry.

Pause.

I'm sorry.

Pause.

Miss, I'm really sorry.

AMANDA *turns back to* CHRIS.

Miss?

Silence.

Miss?

Silence.

Miss?

Silence. CHRIS *motions for* DEE *to go. She does. Silence.*

CHRIS. I didn't tell her to come up here.

AMANDA. It doesn't matter.

CHRIS. They did a stupid thing.

AMANDA. It doesn't matter.

Silence.

CHRIS. When you get back into the classroom, you'll feel better.

Pause.

Don't you think?

Pause.

Amanda?

AMANDA. I'm not going back in the classroom.

CHRIS. Don't make any rash decisions.

AMANDA. I'm not coming back.

CHRIS. Take your time. You'll feel differently in a few weeks.

AMANDA. I won't.

CHRIS. You'll –

AMANDA. I won't. I know I won't.

Pause.

CHRIS. What will you do?

AMANDA. I don't know.

CHRIS. You're a brilliant teacher. And you love it. It's obvious to everyone who sees you teach that you love it.

AMANDA. I can't.

CHRIS. Amanda, please.

AMANDA. No.

CHRIS. Please, just say you'll think about it.

AMANDA. No. I can't. No.

The End.

A Nick Hern Book

Mogadishu first published in Great Britain in 2011 as a paperback original by Nick Hern Books Limited, 14 Larden Road, London W3 7ST

Reprinted in this revised edition in 2012

Mogadishu copyright © 2011, 2012 Vivienne Franzmann

Vivienne Franzmann has asserted her right to be identified as the author of this work

Cover image: Savannah Gordon-Liburd (as Dee) and Malachi Kirby (as Jason) in the original 2011 production of *Mogadishu*, photograph by Jonathan Keenan
Cover design: Ned Hoste

Typeset by Nick Hern Books, London
Printed in the UK by CPI Group (UK) Ltd, Croydon, CR0 4YY

A CIP catalogue record for this book is available from the British Library

ISBN 978 1 84842 254 4

CAUTION All rights whatsoever in this translation are strictly reserved. Requests to reproduce the text in whole or in part should be addressed to the publisher.

Amateur Performing Rights Applications for performance, including readings and excerpts, by amateurs in English should be addressed to the Performing Rights Manager, Nick Hern Books, 14 Larden Road, London W3 7ST, *tel* +44 (0)20 8749 4953, *e-mail* info@nickhernbooks.demon.co.uk, except as follows:

Australia: Dominie Drama, 8 Cross Street, Brookvale 2100, *fax* (2) 9938 8695, *e-mail* drama@dominie.com.au

New Zealand: Play Bureau, PO Box 420, New Plymouth, *fax* (6) 753 2150, *e-mail* play.bureau.nz@xtra.co.nz

South Africa: DALRO (pty) Ltd, PO Box 31627, 2017 Braamfontein, *tel* (11) 712 8000, *fax* (11) 403 9094, *e-mail* theatricals@dalro.co.za

United States of America and Canada: The Agency (London) Ltd, see details below

Professional Performing Rights Applications for performance by professionals in any medium and in any language throughout the world (and amateur and stock performances in the United States of America and Canada) should be addressed to The Agency (London) Ltd, 24 Pottery Lane, Holland Park, London W11 4LZ, *fax* +44 (0)20 7727 9037, *e-mail* info@theagency.co.uk

No performance of any kind may be given unless a licence has been obtained. Applications should be made before rehearsals begin. Publication of this play does not necessarily indicate its availability for amateur performance.